Manifest With Ease

Mindful and Effortless Law of Attraction
Techniques With Practical and Actionable
Steps for Personal and Financial Success

Jana Alonso Bartlett, Kim Le

Contents

Foreword

My name is Sandra, and I've known Jana for years, long before she created the School of Integrative Healing and found success in her business. I got really interested in her work when I saw her life take off in ways that seemed almost magical, especially with her health and wealth.

Before working with Jana, I was stuck in a rut, and my business was struggling. I wanted to participate in one of her programs but I was hesitant to take the leap to invest in myself. Fortunately, I won a spot in one of Jana's mini-training programs called the Energetic Accelerator, which was all about using intentional practices to manifest your desires. We did daily gratitude exercises, money journaling, and learned how to enter an alpha brainwave state to reprogram our minds for success.

At that time, my partner and I were living in an Airbnb, struggling to find an affordable place to move to. We needed a car and a new laptop but had a tight budget. I also wanted to join the School of Integrative Healing. Our list of needs was long, but the money wasn't there.

Within three weeks of doing the Energetic Accelerator course, everything shifted. Manifestations started pouring in. We received enough money to pay for a full membership to the School of Integrative Healing. We found a car in perfect condition for one-third of our budget from the neighbor next door. My partner got his laptop. Our life was changing so quickly and dramatically that I was amazed. To add to it all, in the same incredible week, we even got a call about a beautiful flat we wanted years ago but couldn't get. The landlord offered it to us out of the blue, and we negotiated a lower rent!

Two practices I learned through the School of Integrative Healing, and use daily are the alpha brainwave meditation, founded by Jose Silva and Rapid Resolution Therapy (RRT), founded by Dr. Jon Connolly. Alpha brainwave meditation helps reduce stress, enhance creativity, and improve mental clarity by transitioning your brain from active thinking to a relaxed, aware state. RRT is a therapeutic approach that quickly resolves emotional and psychological issues using hypnosis, guided imagery, and cognitive-behavioral techniques.

Fast forward a few years, and I'm now working towards a certification from the School of Integrative Healing. My business is thriving and breaking records regularly. I can't express enough gratitude for the abundance my partner and I continue to experience thanks to Jana and her teachings. Life just flows so much easier now.

If you are reading this, you must feel what I once felt. There must be a part of you that is not completely satisfied with life. Then let me assure you, you are in the right place. Like me, you manifested this opportunity, and only you can take it to the next level. It all starts with a decision to want change, to want more. If you commit yourself to the path, these are the right tools and people to support you on your journey so you, too, can take that quantum leap to where all your dreams will be answered. This journey has only just begun; be excited for what's next!

- Living life intentionally, Sandra Mappa,

Introduction

My name is Jana, pronounced "Hannah", but with a "J" like in jalapeno because my mum was Spanish. My dad wanted to call me "Anna," but my mum wanted it to feel Spanish, so "Jana" with a "J" was born. My name does not exist in Spain or England, so as you can imagine school, banks, paperwork, generally introducing myself has been a real treat. At least people don't forget me, hey.

I am an integrative healing expert, investor, speaker, teacher, author, former contributor on Good Morning Spain, human, partner, pit bull lover, and founder of the School of Integrative Healing. Integrative healing is the concept of multimodality and multidimensional healing. I believe in a complete holistic multidimensional approach because humans are multidimensional in nature. Science is now showing what has been known by ancient traditions for centuries: that humans are not just the physical body. You have to consider the fact that you are also energy, mind, emotions, and spirit, or the healing will not work fully. This is my mission, my life's purpose. Let me tell you why.

In 2011, I found myself at a crossroads. Faced with seemingly insurmountable challenges, I was diagnosed with severe depression, social anxiety, and an eating disorder in the same three weeks my mum was diagnosed with cancer. The seven years that followed were her learning how to die while I learned how to live truly for the first time. It was the profound decision to take things into my own hands instead of following others' limited advice that turned my life around. It was not magic but the power of focused intention and belief, together with trauma release, embodiment, and shamanism, that transformed my reality. I saw my mum pass away at the age of 56, and I realized that it is so easy to take this life for granted until it's too late and that what I could regret not doing was a far scarier prospect than trying and failing on the way. This pivotal experience ignited a passion within me to educate millions of people on what is possible if you truly do the inner work and commit to your healing.

This book, in particular, will focus on using the law of attraction and the science of manifestation to create the life of your dreams. "Manifest With Ease" is more than just a book; it is a practical guide inspired by one of the most popular programs I offer, called Manifest With Ease: 5 Day Challenge.

Full disclosure: due to my dyslexia (my greatest superpower), I have chosen more of a conversational style, so forgive my imperfect and intentional writing style for authenticity's sake.

The program and this guide were designed to demystify the science of manifestation. I aim to make these principles accessible and actionable for you, particularly addressing the unique challenges and aspirations that you face as a human being. This book blends rigorous scientific research with timeless spiritual wisdom to give you a balanced, understandable approach to a subject that can often seem esoteric: manifestation.

Manifestation is not just about wishful thinking. Despite common misconceptions, it is not a mere fantasy. Many believe it requires special powers or a secret key held only by the fortunate few. In these pages, I will debunk these myths, clarifying how manifestation is a power that lies within you, just by the fact that you are a living human being.

My mission is simple: to empower you to tap into your inherent ability to shape your destiny. The principles that govern the universe are more intertwined with your personal life than you might initially believe. Through my journey and extensive research, I have seen firsthand how mastering these principles can lead to profound changes in happiness, love, success, and financial well-being.

I invite you to approach this book with an open heart and a willing mind. Embrace the exercises and insights and commit to the daily practices. In addition, each chapter ends with a link to additional online training and practical hands-on belief clearing, meditation, journaling, and other practices that will enhance your ability to manifest. Remember, the consistency of your actions will fuel your success. Let this be the moment you step into a life of abundant possibilities—a life where you, too, can manifest ridiculous results in happiness, love, success, wealth, or whatever your goal may be, intentionally and with ease. It's time to leave struggle, burnout, and all that behind.

The Science Of Manifestation

How Your Thoughts Shape Reality

Have you ever heard of how thoughts can create your reality? It almost sounds like something out of a science fiction novel, doesn't it?

In this chapter, I will explore the science behind the "woo" and show you that this isn't a made-up science fiction novel but the world that you are living in. This is not about turning you into a physicist. Instead, it is to enhance your understanding and help you build belief in the idea that your mind and your being hold incredible power over the material world. By the end of this chapter, the concept of using your thoughts to influence your reality will not just be limitless and magical thinking—it will be a grounded strategy backed by science.

Exploring The Observer Effect

In the realm of quantum physics, there is a phenomenon known as the observer effect. It suggests that the mere act of observing a particle can change its behavior.

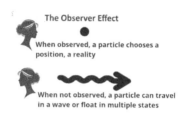

The Observer Effect

When observed, a particle chooses a position, a reality

When not observed, a particle can travel in a wave or float in multiple states

Imagine a particle going through life as a wave of possibilities. It floats through existence in multiple states simultaneously—until it is observed. Once you look, it chooses a position, a reality. Now, translate this to your life: your focused attention and intention might actually help pinpoint a possibility out of your wave of dreams and aspirations, turning it into reality. It's like looking through a sea of potential futures, and depending on where you direct your focus, your observations bring your potential future to life.

Wave-particle Duality and Thoughts

Wave-particle duality is another mind-bending concept from quantum mechanics. Particles like photons or electrons can behave both as particles and as waves. This means they have the potential to exist in multiple states at once until a definite state is observed. Now, think of your thoughts as similar to these particles. Each thought holds a range of potential outcomes, simultaneously existing in many possible futures. When you focus your thoughts intensely, you're basically observing one of those possibilities, collapsing all other potential states into one defined reality. This is how focused intention and being can help manifest specific outcomes in your life.

Entanglement And Connectivity

Quantum entanglement is a remarkable phenomenon where particles become interconnected, and the state of one (no matter how far apart) can instantaneously affect the state of another. Apply this concept to manifestation, and you can see how your thoughts and feelings might be intertwined with the universe itself—your inner state influencing your external reality. Just as entangled particles remain connected across vast distances, your connection with the universe can help dictate your life experiences through synchronous events and coincidences that align with your emotional and mental energy.

Manifestation and Cause and Effect

What is manifestation? Manifestation is a universal law. It is the process where your thoughts and energy become physical reality and matter, and **it is always happening** (whether or not you believe in it). It always works because it's a law of the universe, just like gravity is. You would look at someone strangely if they told you gravity didn't work for them; well, it is *actually* the same as saying manifestation doesn't work for you. Maybe you just haven't yet mastered the ability to do it consciously, but that's a different story, and that's why you have this book.

Manifestation doesn't just turn on when you are trying to manifest a house or a relationship. Manifestation is a science of cause and effect. Your thoughts and energy are the cause, and the effects are your actions and external reality. Your current external reality is *always* a match to or a mirror of your past internal reality. It does not matter how aware of the process you are; you are still creating everything that shows up in your life. Therefore, you must take 100% responsibility for everything in life because you created it, consciously or unconsciously. This is really fabulous because if you are the problem 100% of the time, then you are also the solution.

Keep reading, and I will answer the question, *"Why would I create something that I don't want??"* That's a really great question and should be answered. But for now, let's look at a real-life example of manifestation in action. Let's talk about the story of Dr. Joe Dispenza, a scientist, teacher, and lecturer renowned for using his mind to heal his spine. In 1986, at 23 and the pinnacle of his chiropractic career, Joe Dispenza was struck by a truck while biking in a triathlon. Doctors informed him that he might never walk again, having sustained six compressed vertebrae from the accident, recommending radical spine surgery. Instead of following their advice, he left the hospital and committed himself to healing his spine using his mind.

Joe turned to meditation and visualization techniques to rewire his brain, picturing his body becoming whole again. As a chiropractor, he visualized how the fractured vertebrae needed to be realigned. He devoted two hours each day, twice a day, to this practice. If his focus wavered, he started over, determined that the mental image had to be crystal clear for his body to begin healing. Within just ten and a half weeks, he could stand on his own. Joe Dispenza achieved what some might call miracles, but to him, it simply affirmed the belief that *"The power that made the body, heals the body."*

As demonstrated in this example, your concentrated thought and visualization processes can guide your actions and decisions toward realizing your goals. Imagine you want to run a marathon. You start by picturing yourself crossing the finish line, feeling all the excitement and pride. This focused thinking starts to guide your everyday choices. You might start waking up earlier to train, eating healthier, or joining a running club. All these little decisions, influenced by your visualization, bring you closer to your goal.

In simple terms, it's like how observing a particle in quantum mechanics stabilizes its state. Your consistent mental focus acts like an observer, helping to make your goal a reality. This visualization becomes a guiding light, leading your everyday actions—no matter how small or unrelated they seem—toward actually finishing that marathon.

By delving into these principles, you've gained knowledge and the power to shape your world. Remember, the universe communicates through thoughts, intentions, and connections. In the upcoming sections, I will continue to explore how you can improve on this and effect the changes you desire in your life.

Neuroplasticity and You: How to Rewire Your Brain for Success

Neuroplasticity might sound like a complex scientific term, but it has a huge impact on your life. Simply put, neuroplasticity is the brain reorganizing itself by forming new neural connections throughout life. It's like rewiring your brain. This means that your brain is not fixed by your genetics or early childhood experiences; it's constantly changing based on what you learn and experience every day. This is fantastic news if you're looking to improve your life through manifestation, as it means you can rewire your brain to support your goals and dreams.

When you repeatedly think of specific thoughts or perform certain actions, your brain forms and strengthens pathways that make these thoughts and actions more *effortless* and *natural*. It is like walking through a field of tall grass. The first time you walk through, you must push your way, but each subsequent pass flattens the grass further, making the path clearer and easier to travel. Similarly, when you consistently focus on positive thoughts and self-image and visualize your goals as if you've already achieved them, you're creating new neural pathways that support a mindset perfect for manifestation. This is why habits—both good and bad—are so powerful. They form patterns in your brain that influence your behavior, often subconsciously.

You can use several effective techniques to enhance neuroplasticity and harness its power for successful manifestation, which I'll talk about in later chapters. Meditation, for example, is a wonderful practice for this purpose. One form of meditation is sitting quietly, paying attention to your thoughts, feelings, and sensations in the present moment without judging them. This practice helps reduce stress and trains your brain to stay focused on the present, making it easier to keep your intentions clear without getting distracted by negative thoughts.

Visualization is another powerful tool. By vividly imagining yourself achieving your goal—as if it's *already* happened—you engage your brain in a way that mirrors the real experience. Your brain can't tell the difference between the present, past, or future. Whether you're thinking about something happening now, a past event, or a future goal, it stimulates the same neural regions as if you were actually experiencing it. Over time, these regions get familiar with your desires, and your brain starts working with your goals, spotting opportunities, and taking actions that help make those imagined scenarios real.

Affirmations are also super important for rewiring your brain. They're simple, positive statements that, when repeated often, help you overcome negative thoughts and self-sabotage. If believing in yourself or thinking you're worthy seems like a big leap, it's not. You just need to practice that thought over and over until you believe it, and then you can start making positive changes. Think of affirmations as a workout for your brain, strengthening the pathways that support your goals and weakening the ones that hold you back.

As you integrate these techniques into your daily routine, remember that the key to changing your brain lies in committing to the process and consistently doing the work. You only grow and get extraordinary results if you can be honest with yourself. The schooling system teaches learning is knowing. You go to school, read your books, and do an exam. Then you forget everything that you have just learned. I was a straight-A student and a massive nerd. I loved studying, and no one had to make me do homework. But even though I enjoyed learning, I never remembered anything after my exams. I never implemented it or used it. It never transformed my life.

So, unconsciously, it's expected that you will approach your personal development like you did with your traditional education. Yet, that's not the correct approach, and it won't change your life. Suppose you continue to use the conventional way of learning. In that case, you will be reading books forever, and you will never see the manifestations. I will show you a new way of learning here. The School of Integrative Healing is an online school I created that is the synergy of different modalities, dimensions, and teachers. We guide high achievers, peak performers, and business owners to heal from the inside out and create the most extraordinary of lives. In the school, we teach that learning doesn't just mean knowing something intellectually but implementing it so that it becomes cellular wisdom (actually changes your DNA). You want that information to become a part of your body and who you are, so you do it automatically. Once you have achieved this, you are setting the stage to support yourself in manifesting your desires, transforming *what once seemed like wishful thinking into tangible outcomes.*

I want to share Shakti's story, a client who took the training from the School of Integrative Healing and fully embraced living every moment authentically and intentionally, knowing that *"we are all manifesting ALL the FREAKING TIME."* Like many, Shakti suffered from burnout at work, felt lost, and was unclear about her future when she started her spiritual journey. At that time, she had no concept of what manifestation was. She later discovered yoga and meditation and began training with her yoga teacher, who first introduced her to the idea that life is much more than the physical reality she knew. It was also her yoga teacher who introduced Shakti to my teachings. I was offering a "Manifest With Ease" course, and Shakti came up with every excuse possible, including it being her birthday, not to participate. Her yoga teacher insisted she register, feeling intuitively that it was something she had to do. Shakti joined the School of Integrative Healing immediately after completing the course.

What makes Shakti and her story impressive is that after joining the school, she threw herself almost obsessively into studying as many modalities as she could, attending every workshop and event we offered. She learned to heal trauma, clear trapped emotions, and release limiting beliefs. Two practices she still does every single day without fail are journaling and gratitude work. Her dedication paid off, allowing her to master the ability to identify and shift things within herself as they come up, enabling her goals and dreams to manifest. Before joining the School of Integrative Healing, her dream was to build a private yoga practice of her own. She struggled to find the "perfect" strategy to launch her yoga business, which at the time only had two clients paying €20 per class. She said all she hoped for was to earn enough just to cover her expenses, not believing she could have anything more. A few months after joining the School of Integrative Healing, her business started to take off, and she made €80K in her first year. Shakti was implementing what she was learning, making it part of her DNA, and she was starting to see results.

Here are a few examples of her conscious manifestations over the last couple of years. Before one of her meditation practices, she told herself, "I will have €10k when I open my eyes." After her meditation, she opened her eyes and saw a client had registered for one of her €10k programs. In another instance, she went swimming and focused on the intention of gaining a new client for her program. When she came out of the pool, she saw a client had just joined her program as intended.

In one of my recent workshops, I asked Shakti what her next goal was, and she said, "22 in 22." I asked her what that meant, and she explained she wanted to earn €22k in 22 days, something she had never done before. After the 22 days were up, I followed up with her and asked how much she had earned. Guess what number it came to after she tallied up all her sources of revenue and completed the currency conversions to euro? EXACTLY €22k. And the list goes on...

The Psychology Behind Belief Systems And Their Impact On Manifestation

Your beliefs are incredibly powerful, especially when it comes to your belief around your self-image (a fancy way of saying the inner mental picture of your identity stored in the unconscious mind). They shape your view of the world and dictate your behavior, often unconsciously. Think about it: the deeply ingrained belief that you are capable and worthy can drive you to apply for that job you have always wanted, ask for a well-deserved raise, ask someone out on a date, or even start a new venture. Conversely, if you believe that success is for others but not for you, that belief alone can stop you, no matter how skilled or prepared you might be. This is the cornerstone of manifestation: *what you genuinely believe materializes in your life.* This is because your beliefs influence your decisions, actions, and reactions. They create a filter through which you perceive and respond to the world, attracting experiences that mirror back to you and reinforce those very beliefs through your external world.

Beliefs are thoughts that have been repeated many times, so they don't necessarily have to be true, even if they feel true to you. These mental biases are shortcuts that your brain uses to quickly process information and make decisions. To illustrate this, let's consider learning to drive a car. When you first start, all the different tasks can feel complex and challenging to coordinate. However, with practice, it becomes easier and more natural until it becomes automatic. You can even drive and sing along to your favorite songs without a problem. Beliefs work in a similar way. They are like automatic thoughts that have become ingrained in your thinking. And if you really want to stretch your mind, your self-image or identity is essentially a collection of thoughts about yourself that have become an automatic program, which you *perceive* as the real you.

While these biases help to process information more *efficiently*, they can also skew your perception of reality and limit your potential. For example, confirmation bias leads you to pay more attention to information that confirms your pre-existing beliefs and dismisses what contradicts them. If you *believe you* are unlucky, you are more likely to notice and remember when things go wrong. This reinforces your belief and brings more bad luck into your reality. This can create a negative cycle, where negative expectations prevent you from taking risks or seizing opportunities, thus perpetuating the experiences that confirm your original belief.

One striking example of how powerful belief can be is the placebo effect. In this well-documented medical phenomenon, people experience fundamental changes in their health simply because they believe they are receiving treatment, even if they are not. The treatment they had been given had no therapeutic effect. The changes these people experienced were not merely "all in the mind"—they were *real*, physiological changes triggered by belief. Similarly, when you practice manifestation, your thinking and belief that specific outcomes will occur can set in motion everything needed to bring those outcomes to fruition.

Building new belief systems to support your goals and desires is essential for effective manifestation. The initial step involves identifying and challenging limiting beliefs that may hinder your progress. In my work with shamanic medicine, I draw on teachings that have endured for millennia. Shamans emphasize that life mirrors our internal reality—a continuous *feedback loop*. Understanding this principle was pivotal in transforming my own life outcomes.

Back in 2018, during my shamanic training, one of the issues I chose to work on was relationships. I had been stuck in a painful cycle for four years, consistently attracting men who were not interested in committing to me. At the time, I was desperate for love, and with my mum's declining health, I felt a deep sense of insecurity. I *mistakenly* believed that falling in love could rescue me from the pain I was experiencing.

To address this, I began applying the concept of life as a feedback loop, where my experiences were the effects, and I was the cause. I embarked on a journey to uncover the inner reasons behind my repeated attraction to commitment-phobic partners. After a particularly difficult breakup, which surprisingly brought more relief than grief, I decided to sit down and honestly examine my thoughts and emotions. It was the first time in my life that I consciously tracked how I had been creating disappointment in my love life.

Through this introspection, I realized that my choice of partners was rooted in a deep-seated belief that I was unlovable. I settled for what I could get because I didn't believe someone could love me. Subconsciously, I kept choosing partners who reinforced this belief. Additionally, I discovered that I held an unconscious belief that love meant sacrificing freedom and fun. I came to understand that *"I am lovable"* or *"love means loss of freedom"* were merely repeated thoughts, not truths. It was time to break free from these limiting beliefs and nurture belief systems that aligned with what I truly desired.

Over the next three months, I focused on cultivating new beliefs such as *"I love myself, and I believe that I can be deeply loved for who I am"* and *"A healthy relationship supports and propels both individuals forward."* I also worked on releasing my attachment to immediate results and practiced patience. Three months later, I met Craig, who is still my partner after four years. Together, we have built a life that we are truly proud of—a life that fuels both our individual desires and paths.

The way life works is that your internal experiences—thoughts, beliefs, frequency, energetic patterns, or ancestral influences— are reflected back to you in your external reality, your life's narrative. Life *isn't* about punishment; instead, it serves as a mirror, revealing aspects within you that require attention and change. This feedback loop provides invaluable insights into areas where personal growth and transformation are needed.

To initiate change, you must observe your own life. You can redirect your focus when faced with undesirable circumstances rather than feeling like a victim of the current circumstances. Remind yourself that you have creative power when you look inside. Instead of asking disempowering questions like, *"Why does nothing ever work out for me?"* You can ask empowering questions such as, *"What within me is a match to what I don't desire in my life?"* or *"What part of me is scared of what I truly desire?"* This shift in inquiry marks the beginning of healing work—the essential process through which life begins to improve.

To effectively program this approach, you must refrain from questioning manifestation or disputing the laws of the universe. Instead, embrace these principles as foundational to your journey toward personal empowerment and fulfillment.

This is a client's story about overcoming her fear of lack of money by letting go of old beliefs.

"A friend introduced me to the Manifest With Ease material, which turned out to be exactly what I needed. My life had always been about doing the responsible thing and meeting everyone's expectations. I was stunned when Jana said that to get what I wanted, I had to "die to myself." I instantly realized that the training and Jana herself were manifestations of my desires, guiding me toward the quantum leaps I craved. To live authentically and create the life I wanted, I needed to "die" or rather let go of my old life and beliefs and embrace a new way of living and thinking. And that's exactly what I did.

I immersed myself in the training and connected deeply with Jana's relatable and passionate approach, which made the insights really stick for me. One exercise that was transformative involved journaling the stories I had been telling myself and rewriting them to craft a new narrative. This exercise completely shifted my mindset. I recently decided to leave my six-figure corporate job, which was causing burnout. Instead, I wanted to create passive wealth through something I loved.

Unfortunately, it wasn't long before fear, anxiety, and doubt started creeping into my mind. I started to question whether I had made the right decision. Money was leaving, and none was coming in. Fortunately, through the exercises, I discovered that I had been subconsciously feeding myself negative messages, which caused my fears and kept me stuck living a life I didn't desire. I was subconsciously telling myself that I was only capable of earning income as a corporate employee and that passive income streams were rare and nearly impossible to succeed in. Over time, by rewriting this story and rewiring my brain, I replaced my old beliefs with new ones that were more aligned with my desires. Understanding that my previous beliefs were just made-up stories that I could change helped me overcome the fear and anxiety. As those negative feelings started to dissolve, my energy and vibration started to become aligned with new ideas and opportunities. So many opportunities were presented to me, many of which had not even been on my radar. I am now happily pursuing a passive revenue stream that I love."

Epigenetics: How Your Environment Shapes Your Genes

Dr. Bruce Lipton, a cellular biologist, was born into the traditional model and thinking of life and gene theory. The prevailing belief was that we are all victims of circumstance and genetics, unable to create our own lives. If someone's destiny was to be unhappy, they were believed to be destined for perpetual unhappiness. This model fostered beliefs such as "*I'm just a depressed person,*" "*I'm not meant to be wealthy,*" or "*I'm incapable of sustaining a relationship; I'm meant to be alone.*" These entrenched scientific ideas made it challenging to envision a different reality.

However, Bruce Lipton challenged this *incomplete* theory by delving into epigenetics, a quantum science that asserts the environment—composed of beliefs and energy—shapes genes rather than genes determining our fate. In his book, *The Biology of Belief*, Lipton argues that genes are not predetermined. Thus, regardless of the life one has lived up to this point, changing the environment can enable individuals to create lives aligned with their desires. He asserts that we are not victims but rather *masters of our destinies*, capable of creating lives abundant in peace, happiness, and love.

Reflecting on his personal journey, Lipton reveals that when he first entered biology, he was unhappy, facing financial difficulties and a divorce. He believed he was destined for perpetual misery in the traditional scientific paradigm, even thinking he possessed a "miserable gene." However, realizing he could shape his own life, he now travels the world teaching this "new biology." He reflects, "

> *Instead of slowing down with age, I feel more and more energized by the life I have created, the connections I have made, and those who are also dedicated to creating a more harmonious planet. I continue to enjoy the honeymoon that I am having with Margaret, who is my best friend, my life partner, and my love. In short, my life is so much richer and so much more satisfying that I no longer ask myself if*

I could be anybody, who would I be? For me, the answer is a no-brainer. I want to be me."

What Are Vibrational Frequencies And How Do They Affect Manifestation?

Understanding vibration and energy frequencies may seem like entering a physics classroom. Yet, it is a profoundly important concept that influences every moment of your life. Imagine everything about you is emitting specific energy frequencies. These frequencies are akin to radio waves from a station; just as tuning into the right radio frequency allows you to catch your favorite song, aligning your energy vibrations with your desires attracts similar experiences and opportunities into your life.

This concept is not merely poetic; it is rooted in the Law of Attraction, which states that similar energies attract each other. For example, emitting the feeling of wealth (the wealth radio station) draws abundant outcomes and experiences, while feeling continual feelings of not having enough (never enough radio station) attracts experiences of not having enough. Scientific research supports the idea that human energy fields can impact the environment and relationships. Studies reveal that the heart emits an electromagnetic field that varies with emotions, detectable by those around you. This field can synchronize with others, possibly explaining why certain people evoke strong vibes—good or bad. It also clarifies why you feel more drawn to some individuals than others. Realizing your energy extends beyond your physical self and affects people and things around you underscores the importance of managing the energy you emit.

For example, a joyful person often attracts other joyful people and experiences through visible behaviors and energy frequencies that create a magnetic pull. In terms of manifestation, moving beyond the conventional ideas of positive and negative is beneficial. Manifestation involves aligning with a specific frequency—it simply "is" rather than being inherently positive or negative, as human perceptions define it. These labels may limit your understanding and may not always serve you well.

Discussing positivity and negativity in this context is more about clarifying what you desire or don't desire in life rather than categorizing things as inherently good or bad. This work focuses on bringing unconscious patterns into awareness, enabling you to transform what you don't like into what you do like.

A remarkable example of this concept is the story of how I met Craig (my partner) and Tamsin (my work wife). Believe it or not, we all attended the same gym in Malaga for nearly two years without crossing paths. It was only after I had done significant inner work on my relationships, addressed my beliefs about being lovable, and developed a strong sense of self-security that I finally met Craig. I was now emitting a different frequency, one of openness and security in love rather than neediness.

To make it even more incredible, during those two years at the gym, Craig was not open to a serious relationship. He was only seeking casual connections. However, something shifted for him the year we met, and he made the decision that he was ready to find his life partner. A few weeks later, we crossed paths and couldn't seem to stop bumping into each other. When we were on different "radio stations" or frequencies, it was as if we lived in different realities within the same city. But when we were on the same frequency, it felt like we couldn't avoid encountering each other.

The story with Tamsin is similar. She was a friend of my sister's and also trained at the same gym, yet we never met until after the quarantine in 2020. It's interesting to note the timing of our meeting. That year, Tamsin had been in the hospital and declared to the universe that she never wanted to experience that again. She was actively searching for new opportunities in work and health and was truly ready for change. It was around the same time that I came up with the idea of the School of Integrative Healing and was seeking support from people who believed in this work. The frequency Tamsin held was "*I am ready for inner change*" and "*I need a new job*," while I was looking for assistance from individuals who resonated with my work. Since then, our partnership has been incredibly strong and supportive.

The next question that naturally arises is, "*How can I change my frequency to attract more of what I desire?*" Firstly, your emotions serve as indicators of the frequency you are currently holding. If you feel fear whenever you spend money, it signifies that you are tuned into the radio station of lack. If you find yourself becoming upset and thinking, "*Everyone is in a relationship except me*," when you see couples kissing on the street, it means you are **not** on the radio station of romantic love. But don't worry, just as thoughts and beliefs can be changed, so can your vibration. In fact, it's quite simple when you know how.

There are several daily practices that can assist you in shifting your frequency. Starting your day with gratitude for what you already have is particularly powerful, as it tunes you into the radio station of abundance. By shifting from a mindset of lack or discontent to one of abundance and appreciation, you can significantly elevate your vibration. One effective method is to acknowledge and write down what you are grateful for or reflect on a recent positive experience. This shift in mindset not only impacts your emotions but also has a tangible effect on what you attract into your life. Practicing gratitude can transform an ordinary day into a series of fortunate events simply because you began on a note noticing everything you already have.

The Role Of The Subconscious Mind In Manifestation

Imagine your mind as an iceberg. What you see above the water represents your conscious mind, the part you know and use to make everyday decisions. But below the water lies a much larger mass, the subconscious. This vast and powerful aspect of your mind stores all your memories, transgenerational blessings and trauma, beliefs, frequency, impulses, experiences, desires, and accumulated knowledge. Understanding and harnessing the power of your subconscious is crucial in manifestation, as it profoundly influences your reality, often in ways you might not realize.

The subconscious mind operates like a tape player. From early childhood, it begins recording everything that happens to you—every word you hear, every emotion you feel. Over time, these recordings form scripts running in the background, guiding how you think, behave, and make decisions—essentially shaping your inner and outer reality. When these scripts are positive, they empower you to achieve your desires. However, harmful scripts can be barriers, preventing you from manifesting your goals. The challenge, then, is to feed your subconscious with ideas that lead you toward your goals and rewrite those scripts that hold you back.

Accessing the subconscious to align it with your conscious manifestation goals is possible through various techniques. Hypnotherapy, for example, delves deep into the subconscious, allowing you to identify and modify these scripts directly. By reaching a state of deep relaxation, a trained hypnotherapist can help uncover hidden beliefs and reprogram your mind with positive affirmations and suggestions. This process can be incredibly potent in overcoming deep-seated fears and limiting beliefs that may not be accessible through conscious thought alone, which is why we regularly use it in the School of Integrative Healing.

Subliminal messages offer another avenue for subconscious transformation. Whether auditory or visual, these messages operate below the level of conscious awareness but are perceived subconsciously. By repeatedly exposing yourself to positive, affirming messages, you can begin to alter underlying beliefs and attitudes, planting seeds for change that grow over time.

Alpha Brainwave Meditation, founded by Jose Silva, also provides a direct connection to the subconscious. Through regular practice, you clear mental clutter and create a calm, receptive space where you can consciously plant thoughts aligned with your desires. Alpha Brainwave Meditation directly allows you to prepare the "soil" of your unconscious mind, making it fertile for intentions and affirmations to take root and manifest.

The impact of subconscious beliefs on your reality cannot be overstated. These beliefs can silently sabotage manifestation efforts, operating without your conscious awareness. For example, a subconscious belief that *"money is the root of all evil"* might manifest as procrastination or self-sabotage in financial matters or feeling deep disrespect and disregard for those who are wealthy. To change your reality, you must identify and understand these hidden beliefs, actively transforming them with supportive beliefs that align with your goals.

This transformation highlights a critical point: the subconscious mind is both a repository of your past and a powerful force for shaping your future. By understanding its role in manifestation and learning to modify its deep-seated patterns, you unlock a powerful tool for personal change. Whether through hypnotherapy, subliminal messages, meditation, or another modality, techniques to access and influence the subconscious vary and can be tailored to your preferences and lifestyle. Consistency and a willingness to explore your own mind are essential.

At this stage, let's get serious about manifestation. To make it work for you, you must be honest and fully embrace the belief that beliefs and thoughts create your reality. Ask yourself: *do you honestly believe this? If so, would you continue thinking half of the thoughts you do now, knowing they shape your reality?* Building this belief is foundational to consciously manifesting your life. It eliminates anxiety and fear, knowing you are the creator of your reality and that your wealth consciousness determines your financial outcomes.

Let's build this belief together, grounded in the science of creating a better life. Older scientists, once skeptics, have come to understand through empirical evidence that manifestation is real. Let's embrace this understanding and empower ourselves to manifest our desires with clarity and confidence. But first, you must know what you really want.

EXERCISE:

Journal on, and sit with, "What do I really want?"

- NOT: "What do I want that I think is possible?"

- NOT: "What do other people think I should want?"

- NOT: "What do I want because it is socially acceptable?"

What do YOU really want? You cannot manifest what you want without knowing what it is.

For today's homework, find a piece of paper and journal on *"What do I really want?"* Asking this helps you get clear on your deepest desires and values. It guides you to align your actions with your true self, empowering you to set meaningful goals and make plans that resonate with who you are. This question encourages personal growth by pushing you to challenge any self-imposed limits and live a more authentic and fulfilling life based on what truly matters to you.

Write your responses in the present tense and claim it as if it is already happening now. Do not limit yourselves to doubtful thinking like "I do not think that is possible." Do not even think about whether it is possible. Right now, you're just playing.

Additional Training Available:

I can only provide so much information in this book. However, practicing these concepts and techniques is the real key to successfully manifesting your desires. That's why, at the end of each chapter, I've included links to some pre-recorded workshops from the School of Integrative Healing to support you further on your journey to easily manifest your dreams. Scan the QR Code or enter the link into your browser to access the FREE training. If you already have an account you can log in using the link that was provided in your welcome email.

https://manifestwitheasebook.com

Cultivating Your Manifestation Mindset

I magine holding a garden hose, watering the lush plants of your dream garden—each representing your deepest desires and aspirations. Now, imagine that the water pressure suddenly drops. You check and find a kink in the hose—this is akin to the limiting beliefs or inner block that disrupt the flow of your manifestation efforts. As you would smooth out the hose to restore water flow, identifying and overcoming your limiting beliefs or inner blocks restores the positive energy flow necessary for manifesting your dreams. Let's explore how to identify these kinks, understand their origins, and effect

ively straighten them out to ensure a steady stream of manifestation.

Overcoming Skepticism: Scientific Evidence Supporting Manifestation

Whenever I talk about manifestation, skepticism often comes up. It makes sense—thinking that your thoughts can change reality sounds pretty out there to people who are used to a strictly rational view of the world. But there's a growing amount of scientific evidence that backs up practices like meditation, visualization, and positive thinking, which are key to manifestation. Let's check out some studies and credible sources that provide solid evidence, showing that this stuff is more than just wishful thinking.

One of the most well-documented and widely accepted practices in scientific circles is meditation. Numerous peer-reviewed studies have shown that regular meditation can significantly improve mental health, stress reduction, and overall well-being.

A study published in the *Journal of Cognitive Enhancement* found that participants who engaged in regular mindfulness meditation showed improvements in attention, memory, and emotional regulation. These benefits directly contribute to a person's ability to manifest by fostering a focused, positive mindset attuned to recognizing and seizing opportunities. This is not just about feeling good but about creating a mental environment where positive changes are more likely to occur.

Visualization, another essential practice in manifestation, has also received considerable support from the scientific community. Athletes, for example, have long used visualization techniques to enhance their performance in sports. A study in the *Journal of Sport & Exercise Psychology* reported that athletes who employed visualization techniques significantly improved their physical abilities, even when the physical practice was impossible. This suggests that the mind's ability to simulate reality can prepare the body and psyche to act in ways that align with those visualized scenarios, essentially priming individuals for success in real-world applications.

Positive thinking, often viewed with skepticism, has benefits rooted in psychological research. The concept of a *self-fulfilling prophecy* is well-recognized in psychology and demonstrates how positive expectations can lead to positive outcomes. Furthermore, research in the field of psychoneuroimmunology has shown how a positive outlook can improve health outcomes by boosting the immune system. This intersection of psychology and physiology provides a compelling argument for how the quality of your thoughts can influence the quality of your health and experiences.

These examples really show that manifestation isn't just some wild idea—it's backed by real research. They prove that your thoughts, beliefs, and mental habits can actually shape your reality in measurable ways. As I dig deeper into the science behind manifestation, it will become more evident that using these practices in your daily life can lead to major personal changes and results. I encourage you to see and use these tools not as mystical mumbo jumbo, but as practical methods to boost your well-being and achieve your goals.

How To Bend Time And Leap To Your Goals

How do you take everything you learned and understand about manifestation and apply it effortlessly and easily to your wants and dreams? That is the question that I am going to answer now. Let us tie this all together.

Examine the following diagram. This is how most have been taught to go for your dreams, goals, and desires. This is the old-school method. You are this delightful little DOT at the bottom. The DOT at the top represents you living the life that you want to live, with all the money that you want, with the perfect relationships that you want; this is you with the best health that you desire to have and anything else that you put on your list:

Step By Step to get to the goal at the top:

Society insists that to move from the bottom dot to the top dot you must scale a metaphorical mountain—a linear, arduous, step-by-step journey to success. Many of you unconsciously adopt this approach to your goals, and it often turns out to be the longest, most challenging route you could take. If you desire extraordinary results quickly, this method will not be your best choice.

I often see this illustrated when I ask people to set financial goals. For instance, if someone sets a goal of earning $100,000 a year, they immediately start calculating how much they need to earn each month: $10,000 in January, $10,000 in February, and so on. They map out this linear path to achieving their goal, which seems logical. However, they spiral into self-doubt and disappointment when January or February passes without hitting their target. This reaction is understandable because you have been conditioned to believe that success follows a linear trajectory.

But success does not have to unfold that way. Suppose you want to enjoy the process and achieve results that seem miraculous to others. In that case, erasing this linear mindset from your conscious and unconscious thought patterns is key.

I'm here to guide you on how to achieve your goals using quantum principles, tapping into the exponential possibilities available to you right now. You will learn how to manipulate time and broaden your mindset. You will learn how to achieve outcomes that defy conventional understanding—where three months ago, you did not have the money, the relationship, or whatever else you desired. People will ask you, *"How did you get so lucky?"* But it's not luck; it's science.

Consider the example of Apple, the tech giant that made history in 2023 by reaching a market capitalization of $3 trillion. Their approach to growth was not linear; a significant portion of their revenue surge occurred within the first six months of that year. This example shows that those with substantial wealth understand something most people do not—they leverage strategies that lead to exponential growth.

To achieve such results, you need to break free from the limitations of linear thinking and embrace non-logical, non-linear approaches. In the linear model, the path to success often appears daunting, causing many to hesitate or procrastinate. People postpone starting because the mountain seems too steep. Moreover, those who embark on this path often focus on external actions rather than addressing internal alignment.

In business circles, I often come across individuals who are taught the same strategies, yet their results vary significantly. Why? The difference lies in their inner worlds—their beliefs, mindset, and alignment with their goals. A mere teaching strategy is insufficient; true success necessitates an internal transformation that aligns with external actions.

Therefore, you must align your internal and external worlds to achieve extraordinary results. By shifting away from linear thinking, embracing quantum possibilities, and transforming your inner beliefs, you create fertile ground for rapid, exponential growth in all areas of life. This shift is not just about achieving goals; it is about fundamentally altering how you perceive and engage with success, creating a paradigm where success is not a distant mountain peak but an attainable reality here and now.

Now, I introduce the quantum model of ascertaining your goals, which looks like this:

There is no line in this model, no mapping out an exhaustive and never-ending path toward your goals. The mountain isn't outside of you; the mountain is inside of you. Consider focusing on becoming the version of yourself that is a match with the ultimate destination—the version of you that already possesses what you desire. In other words, shift your focus away from the external, physical world. Instead, turn inward and concentrate on your inner world—the energy you emit, your thoughts, and your emotions. Become the person internally who aligns perfectly with your desired goals. Think the thoughts they would, practice holding the frequency they would hold, and start contemplating the habits and actions they would take. Then take action from this place. As a byproduct of this decision, you will draw in all the necessary circumstances, people, and opportunities along the way.

Stop wasting time trying to force, struggle, or manipulate your external circumstances. The journey towards your goals is not solely about taking action but primarily about internal transformation. This shift in mindset and being is what propelled me from financial struggle to stacking savings and from sharing a tiny flat to renting a €5.1 million house within 3 years—all achieved by changing my inner world and then taking action from that place.

King Richard is an exceptional example of this approach (if you haven't seen the movie, I highly recommend it as it will transform your perspective on manifestation). "King Richard" made a conscious decision that his two daughters, Venus and Serena Williams, would become tennis stars long before they were even born. Throughout their entire childhood, he unwaveringly held onto this clear vision, disregarding any doubts or criticisms from others. As the story unfolded, his dream undeniably transformed into reality.

In the following sections of this chapter, I will discuss various methods you can employ to transform your inner world. These methods are designed to help you achieve remarkable results that could reshape your entire life trajectory. They focus on aligning your inner reality with your external aspirations, enabling you to manifest outcomes that may seem beyond reach.

BE, DO, HAVE: The Most Important Equation In Life

This equation I'm about to share is the most important you'll ever encounter. If you grasp and apply what I'm about to reveal, it alone can transform your life. Take this seriously: BE, DO, HAVE.

Many believe achieving wealth or realizing your dreams hinges on external actions and acquiring material things. You might think that when you have the money, you will be wealthy, relax, rest, or love yourself. But that flawed premise of thinking is exactly what is keeping the money away. Or maybe you think that when you have a house, you will finally feel successful. However, understanding the principles of life and how the universe operates teaches the absolute opposite. Waiting to have something before becoming the version of yourself that can achieve your desires means waiting indefinitely, attributing it to fate to console yourself. Just as you cannot deny the law of gravity, consciousness and being supersede everything—our unconscious mind, physical bodies, and entire lives. This is what conscious manifestation entails. So, the formula is as follows, in this exact order: BE, DO, HAVE.

First, BE the version of yourself that matches your desires. What does this mean? Think like someone who is already successful, feel successful (remember that radio station chat we had), and walk like someone who is successful if you want to attract success. DO from that energy, from your being. Your actions always stem from your current state of being, so they can only create more of the current level of results you desire. If you act from a place of fear and lack, then no matter how hard you work or how great the strategy is, you will only amplify those negative states. Acting from a state of success can only create success (think *King Richard*). Action is important, but energy is more so; it is causal. After BE and DO comes HAVE. Notice that having comes last. The physical manifestation is the last thing to appear. First, you change internally, then you start moving differently in the world, and only then do you see the change in your physical world.

So what is the most essential thing that you do after this? Work on your beliefs, change your thoughts, understand frequency, and regulate your emotions. Take action from that place in the absolute certainty that the potential you have selected in the universe is manifesting. It's just a question of time, and someone who trusts and is certain is not in a rush, so you don't have a problem with that.

Building Mental Resilience: Redefine Your Self-Image

What is self-image? This concept is crucial for manifesting anything in your life. Self-image is the unconscious collection of beliefs you hold about yourself. Each of you has a self-identity, which your nervous system, unconscious mind, and conscious mind continuously strive toward. Think of these systems as a sophisticated robot or the most advanced computer ever developed, always oriented toward your self-image. Your self-image is the goal, and everything in you works towards it.

Some individuals seem consistently fortunate, constantly encountering opportunities. This is because they harbor a self-image, an unconscious belief, that they are inherently lucky. Their self-identity revolves around the idea that they attract and flourish in various situations.

Consequently, their actions align with this self-image, manifesting as reality. Conversely, many others accumulate less favorable beliefs about themselves over their lifetimes. For instance, someone who faced academic challenges in childhood may adopt the belief that they are slow learners, shaping their self-image to perpetually struggle and perceive themselves as incapable of winning or succeeding effortlessly. Regardless of their efforts, they might see themselves as unlovable or destined for failure in life.

Tamsin, my assistant, holds a significant role in my life, and you'll hear me mention her frequently. She has been by my side since before I founded the School of Integrative Healing. Initially, Tamsin viewed herself solely as a hairdresser from her past in the UK, and even after moving on from that career, her self-image remained fixed on limitations around wealth and success. She inadvertently constrained herself until she shifted her self-image and released those beliefs, that this too could work for her.

I also once confined myself to a spiritual identity that I associated with a lack of money. Only when I expanded my self-image to encompass spirituality AND wealth could I experience both. Similarly, a client named Jaqueline used to define herself by her anxiety, stating, *"Life is hard for me because I have anxiety and always will."* By *identifying* with anxiety, she integrated it into her self-image, reinforcing a limiting belief. To change this, she didn't need to deny her current reality. She could instead adopt a new self-image of being someone who finds life easy, that she is someone who is resilient to challenge and always trusts the process of life no matter what is happening. This shift in self-image led to less and less anxiety, and she was no longer identifying with it. In fact, she now sees herself as someone who is competent to deal with challenges.

A fascinating study showcased the profound impact of self-image on academic performance. Schoolchildren who had previously struggled, earning grades of D's and below, underwent a therapeutic process aimed at shifting their self-image from failure to success. Surprisingly, without any additional studying or curriculum modifications, these children experienced a remarkable transformation, becoming A students within a matter of months.

What makes this study even more intriguing is the comparison with a control group of children who also earned D's and below. Instead of engaging in self-image work, this control group received additional tuition. However, their grades remained unchanged. This highlights the importance of addressing inner identity and self-perception rather than solely focusing on external factors to motivate children to work harder.

Consider the immense potential you hold but may not realize it due to your current self-conception. Your identity, who you perceive yourself to be, forms the core of transforming your life—this is the essence of manifestation. By shifting your self-image, everything else naturally follows, allowing you to create with ease.

Remember that you have the power to decide who you are and what your self-image will be. You are the author of your life's story, crafting your identity as you see fit. Your identity is not fixed, not even by your genes, so you can keep changing and transforming your life experience.

Identifying And Overcoming Limiting Beliefs

The first step in transforming your beliefs is recognizing those holding you back. It is like being a detective in your mind, examining thoughts and patterns that have gone unquestioned for too long. Start by reflecting on areas of your life where you feel stuck or unsatisfied—your career, relationships, or personal growth. What thoughts repeatedly surface when you think about these areas? Perhaps it is a nagging feeling that you do not deserve success or that true love is not meant for you.

Limiting beliefs are often rooted in early life experiences. They can stem from offhand comments made by influential figures, societal expectations, or challenging events. For instance, if you grew up in a family where money was always tight, you might have absorbed the belief that this will always be your reality too. Understanding where these beliefs come from can diminish their power over you.

Let me give you an example. I used to believe that I had to be perfect, polished, and professional to be successful in business. One day, during a presentation, I had a malfunction with technology where the sound and audio were not working. Imagine if I held myself to such ludicrous standards as if my success depended on being perfect and not human. At that moment, I could have told myself the story that my students now no longer trusted me, creating feelings of pressure, shame, and anxiety. Notice that these are all feelings and thoughts, not truth. My response could have been one of panic, which could have led to me being awkward on camera, and I would then be teaching a very flustered, ungrounded session. If I held myself to the belief that successful people were perfect, I would likely shut myself off to the receptivity of good things and abundance every time I was imperfect or technology glitched. I would probably convince myself I was unworthy to have clients or my desires. It could have led to a downward spiral quickly. That is an example of how a small belief, tiny as it may be, can literally change and transform your reality.

The new me accepts that I can be imperfect. I can be a human being, the fullness of myself, whatever that looks like, and still be wildly successful. I do not attach abundance to whether I was perfect or how I was feeling on that day. That is now one of my core beliefs and the more human I allow myself to be and be seen as, the more money I make and the more successful I am.

I will wrap up this chapter with an exercise to help you overcome your limiting beliefs and cultivate a mindset to achieve your dreams. In this exercise, asking yourself to envision the self-image of the version of you in your goal offers powerful benefits. It helps clarify your aspirations by vividly picturing yourself achieving what you desire, making your goals feel more tangible and real. This exercise also boosts motivation and confidence, aligning your actions with this envisioned self-image, thereby accelerating your progress toward manifesting your dreams. This is the BE part of the BE, DO, HAVE equation.

EXERCISE:

Write out the self-image / inner identity of the version of you in your goal. Things to consider:

- How do they dress?- How do they move?- How do they respond to challenges?- How do they introduce themselves?- What do they believe about themselves?- Who are they?- What habits do they have?- What is the inner chatter they have?

- What is their dominant feeling or frequency?

- What do they do on the weekend?

- How do they speak to themselves?

Additional Training Available:

I hope you are enjoying the book so far. Let's continue to build momentum toward the life that you truly desire. Scan the QR Code or enter the link into your browser to access your FREE training. If you already have an account you can log in using the link that was provided in your welcome email.

https://manifestwitheasebook.com

Review

Make a Difference with Your Review and Unlock the Power of Generosity

People who give without expecting anything in return live longer, happier lives and often find more success. Would you help someone you've never met, even if you never got credit for it?

Who is this person you ask? They're like you. Or, at least, like you used to be. Less experienced, wanting to make a difference, and needing help, but not sure where to look. Our mission is to make the teachings of manifestation accessible to everyone. Everything we do stems from that mission. And, the only way for us to accomplish that mission is by reaching...well...everyone.

This is where you come in. Most people do judge a book by its cover (and its reviews). My ask on behalf of a person struggling to manifest their dreams, someone you've never met: Please help that person by leaving this book a review. Your gift costs no money and less than 60 seconds to make real, but can change a fellow reader's life forever. Your review could help...

...one more small business provide for their community

....one more entrepreneur support their family.

...one more employee get meaningful work.

...one more client transform their life.

...one more dream come true.

All you have to do is, and it takes less than 60 seconds, to leave a review.

Simply scan the QR code below to leave your review:

https://link.manifestwitheasebook.com/PaperReview

Thank you from the bottom of my heart. I'm excited to help you achieve your dreams faster and easier than you can imagine. You'll love the techniques and strategies I'm about to share in the coming chapters.

Now, back to our regularly scheduled programming.

- Your biggest fan, Jana Alonso Bartlett

Practical Manifestation Techniques

I magine starting your day centered and light, excited to attract the desired experiences and outcomes. Or wrapping up your day by setting the stage for peaceful sleep filled with dreams that inspire and rejuvenate. This is not just a luxury reserved for those with ample free time; it is achievable for anyone, including you, no matter how packed your schedule might seem. Actually, the more packed your schedule is, the more you need it, but that's a conversation for another day. In this chapter, I dive into practical manifestation techniques that seamlessly integrate into your daily life, ensuring that even the busiest individuals can effectively harness the power of manifestation.

The Power of Affirmations: Rewriting Your Mental Script

An affirmation is just a thought you keep repeating. You do it all the time, whether you realize it or not. For example, telling your friends, "*It never works out for me in love,*" is an affirmation. Even if you don't want it to be true, you're still putting it out there as if it is. In personal development, affirmations are about consciously repeating positive thoughts until they become ingrained in your brain. To make effective affirmations, they need to be clear, personal, and really connect with what you want and who you want to be. Start by identifying what you truly want—confidence, love, prosperity, or peace. Then, turn these desires into simple, positive, present-tense statements that confirm you can make them happen. For example, instead of saying, "*I do not want to be stressed,*" you could affirm, "*I am embracing calmness and clarity with every breath I take.*" Instead of "*My business is stuck and not going anywhere.*", you could say, "*I have the resilience and creativity to drive my business forward.*" By making this subtle shift in wording, you are changing the direction of your thoughts and actions. Instead of focusing on what you don't want and complaining about it, you are stopping that negative train of thought and initiating a new path toward the destiny you desire.

The magic of affirmations lies not just in their creation but in their repetition. Why? Each repetition embeds the affirmation deeper into your subconscious, reinforcing the belief and making it a part of your internal narrative. Think of it like watering seeds you have planted. Each repetition is a sprinkle of water, and over time, with consistent care, these seeds sprout, grow, and eventually bear fruit. The practice does not require hours; even a few minutes daily can be profoundly impactful. Morning can be an ideal time when the mind is fresh or at night, just before sleep, when the mind is soft and receptive. As you repeat your affirmations, visualize them as accomplished realities, adding a vivid sensory experience to your words. This combination of vivid visualization and repetitive affirmation accelerates the manifestation process, transforming these desires into realities in your subconscious.

Visualization Techniques: Picturing Your Path To Success

Like any skill, visualization can have its challenges. Distraction is a common obstacle, especially when new to the practice. Your mind may wander or need help conjuring up a clear image. This is normal. When you notice your focus drifting, gently guide it back to your visualization without judgment. Regular practice improves your ability to visualize and increases your mind's capacity to focus over extended periods. This builds gradually with practice.

The most effective way to visualize successful scenarios is in a relaxed state. When your brain waves slow down, it becomes easier to reprogram your unconscious mind. However, your mind can be tricky, and when someone tells you to relax, you often end up tensing up and getting frustrated about being tense. This is not very effective and can be compared to a dog chasing its own tail.

Instead, I recommend using visual and sensory cues that clearly communicate to your body what to do. For example, you can imagine that your body is made of lead. Visualize your feet, legs, and entire body becoming heavy like lead. Focus on the sensation of heaviness and let your body sink into a relaxed state. Another technique is to imagine yourself as a puppet on strings, and suddenly someone cuts all of your strings. Ask yourself, what would your body naturally do if it were free from any tension or control? Allow your body to naturally relax and let go of any tension. By using these visual and sensory cues, you can effectively communicate to your body to relax and enter a state where reprogramming your unconscious mind becomes easier.

Sensory cues are more effective than simply telling your body to relax because your body doesn't understand verbal instructions in the same way. Once you are in a relaxed state, it's time to visualize successful scenarios. Practice feeling gratitude in advance for the things you desire, such as a new relationship, an exciting opportunity, or recognition in your career. The more you vividly *see* and *feel* these scenarios, the more they become normalized in your system, increasing the likelihood of them coming true.

You can incorporate this practice into the pause moments in your day, whether you're at the beach, walking your dog, or before you get up. It doesn't have to be complicated or require sitting with your legs crossed. Make it a part of your daily routine and integrate it seamlessly into your day. You don't even have to close your eyes. And remember, you have full permission to daydream. Let your mind wander and explore different possibilities. Daydreaming can be a powerful tool for creative visualization and manifestation, those blissful feelings are your radio station.

I recommend practicing alpha and theta brainwave meditation, a technique developed by Jose Silva. This meditation process has been known to help individuals tap into their extraordinary potential and achieve remarkable results.

Jose Silva initially developed this method after noticing that his children were not performing well in school. Through the practice of alpha and theta brainwave meditation, his children were able to unlock their hidden abilities, such as intuitive knowledge and the ability to anticipate questions before they were asked, amongst other superhuman qualities.

One of Jose Silva's long-term clients gained significant recognition by applying these techniques to win over 5000 contests. Other clients have reported healing health conditions, manifesting their dream homes, and experiencing radical changes in their finances.

The alpha and theta brainwave states are incredibly powerful as they allow individuals to access their unconscious mind consciously. This means that it becomes easier to program new belief systems and desires. These brainwave states also have the potential to trigger self-healing processes within the body.

If you are interested in exploring these meditation techniques further, we have a variety of alpha and theta brainwave meditations available within the School of Integrative Healing.

Combining affirmations with visualization brings a dynamic layer to your practice. As you affirm your statements, conjure up a mental image of the outcome. If your affirmation is about finding love, imagine yourself with a partner, experiencing joy and companionship. Make this image as detailed as possible—where are you going? What are you feeling? Are there any sounds or smells that you can bring to your awareness? *Feel* and experience every detail to your core. Adding *feeling* to the affirmation or visualization is like telling the universe what you want (thought), and then making sure that you are on the right radio station (feeling), making it more powerful. Your brain, remarkably adept at not distinguishing well between vividly imagined scenes and real ones, begins to align your external environment with your internal vision.

Using Gratitude to Amplify Your Manifestation Power

Gratitude is not just a warm feeling—it is a powerful catalyst in the realm of manifestation, influencing your emotional state and your brain's function. Studies in neuroscience have illuminated how gratitude activates areas of the brain associated with dopamine, the *"feel-good"* neurotransmitter. When you practice gratitude regularly, these areas become more active, making the feeling of gratitude and its positive effects more readily accessible. This neurochemical response does not just elevate your mood; it aligns your vibrational energy with the universe's abundance, making you a magnet for more positive experiences. By fostering a *thankful in advance* mindset, you are priming your brain to expect and recognize the good in life, attracting more goodness.

Daily gratitude practices are both simple and profound in their impact. One effective method is maintaining a gratitude journal. Write down things you are grateful for daily, from significant events like job promotions to everyday pleasures like a delicious cup of coffee in the morning. Writing reinforces these positive experiences, embedding them more deeply in your consciousness and gradually shifting your focus from what is lacking to what is abundant. Over time, this shift enhances your well-being and strengthens your manifestation abilities by keeping you attuned to positivity.

Another daily practice is creating and reciting gratitude affirmations. These statements express appreciation and are designed to be spoken aloud or mentally recited daily. For example, affirmations like *"I am grateful for the endless opportunities that unfold in my life,"* or *"I appreciate the love and support I receive daily,"* help cement a mindset of abundance and appreciation. When spoken with emotion and conviction, these affirmations can transform your energetic output, signaling to the universe that you are open and receptive to blessings and success. Creating affirmations expressing gratitude for something you don't yet have can be a powerful practice. By acknowledging and appreciating the desired outcome as if it already exists, you are sending a signal to the universe that it's already yours, thus manifesting it into reality at great speed.

Integrating gratitude with other manifestation techniques enhances their effectiveness exponentially. For instance, when you combine gratitude with visualization, you picture your desired future and deeply feel gratitude for its presence in your life. This adds a powerful dimension to your visualizations, making them more vivid and vibrationally charged. Similarly, when using affirmations, starting with statements of gratitude sets a positive, receptive tone that amplifies the following affirmations. This synergy accelerates the manifestation process and ensures it is infused with joy and satisfaction rather than need or desperation.

By making gratitude a daily practice, you enhance your emotional well-being, fall in love with your life as it is, and set a robust foundation for manifesting your desires. Giving thanks can unlock doors to abundance and success, that force and pure willpower just can't.

This is an example of a client using gratitude and visualization techniques to manifest a new flat more aligned with her aspirations. She wanted to move due to numerous issues with her current residence and had been searching for almost two years. She documented her gratitude for having found a new flat, as if it had already happened. She expressed love and gratitude for a positive relationship with the new landlord, ample space, and the beauty of the flat. Additionally, she affirmed that she possessed the financial means to afford the monthly rent.

Despite her desperate attempts to search for a flat within her price range and dealing with challenging landlords, she maintained her daily practice of gratitude, inner child work, and other related techniques. She simultaneously visualized the new flat and expressed appreciation for her current living situation.

She recalled that when she used only visualization, the manifestation didn't work. She was eventually successful when she combined appreciation for her existing circumstances with visualization of her desired goals. Within two weeks, she discovered an online listing for the ideal flat and promptly contacted the landlord. She now lives in her dream flat, which is within her budget and has a great relationship with the landlords. She realized that the critical element missing in her lengthy manifestation process was gratitude and appreciation for her current living situation while she visualized and planned for the new dream flat.

Journaling Your Future: A Guide to Effective Journaling

Documenting your success can be a valuable part of your manifestation journey. By keeping a journal where you track evidence that your manifestations are working, you strengthen your focus, faith and belief that this is real, and very much happening. This can prevent you from getting caught up in thoughts of why your desires haven't yet manifested or noticing the lack, which can actually push them further away or slow your manifestation journey right down.

To practice this exercise, simply write down everything that is going well in your life or any evidence that you are getting closer to your goals. For instance, if you desire a dream car, take note of the number of times you see that car on the streets and express gratitude for the abundance that is coming to you to purchase the car, no matter how small. Remember, what you focus on grows.

If you find yourself spiraling into negative thoughts about a particular topic, this is actually a positive sign. It means your unconscious mind is revealing the programs and patterns that you need to clear in order to receive what you want. Write these negative thoughts down and rewrite them, just as I did when I wanted to improve my relationships. Sometimes, this may be a sign that you may need to do some deeper inner work and utilize a healing modality to really clear the program at the root (which is what we do in the School of Integrative Healing). Times of anxiety and negative thoughts are actually phenomenal opportunities for huge blessings and rewards if you put in the work to change these programs, and they tend to happen just before receiving something big.

I'm excited to share with you my favorite journaling prompts that can enhance your manifestations. The first prompt is from Melanie Ann Layer's *Alpha Femme* and the second prompt is inspired by Neville Goddard, a renowned figure known for his teachings on the fulfillment of desires. Both of these prompts have been incredibly helpful during challenging moments in both my personal and professional life.

Let's take a journey back to my 30th birthday, which occurred on August 30th, 2022. This day was meant to be a joyous occasion as my entire family had traveled to Ibiza to celebrate with me. I was particularly proud because it was the first time everyone would see my magnificent new villa. However, this birthday didn't go as planned. It's important to note that you don't manifest what you consciously want, but rather what lies within your unconscious mind.

The day before my family arrived, Craig and I reached a critical point in our relationship. We realized that we needed to address certain patterns and dynamics, or else we would have to part ways. On my birthday, it became clear that we were going to separate.

However, the situation became even more challenging. Not only was the separation emotionally painful, but it also meant that I was left solely responsible for paying our rent and whilst also paying my team. At that time, my team was significantly more than it is now because I had worked on bringing in money, but not managing it. So suddenly, I found myself facing an enormous financial burden, with more expenses than I had ever faced together in one month. I was overwhelmed, scared, and filled with frustration. It was difficult to comprehend how life could encompass such contrasting elements - a beautiful home, the presence of my family, a thriving business, and yet, a daunting and unexpected bill, coupled with a heartbreak. It felt like a lot to handle. However, I reminded myself that I possessed the necessary tools to navigate through this challenging time.

To begin, I allowed myself to experience a period of sadness, fear and self-pity for a few days. I recognized that allowing emotions to be felt and expressed is essential in order to prevent them from becoming "stuck" within the body. After this initial phase, I started a daily journaling practice, focusing on two specific questions each morning for the next 30 days.

- *It's a year from now, how do I want to be telling the story? (Alpha Femme)*

This question serves as a reminder that despite facing challenging circumstances, you are not a helpless victim. You have the power to shape the outcome of your story. In my case, I was determined to achieve a record month to cover all my expenses. Additionally, I understood the importance of aligning myself with the kind of relationship I desired, regardless of whether it involved Craig or not. It was necessary to remember I cannot control other people. I only have control over my own alignment and what I am a match to in my life.

I was faced with several challenges, and it was essential to swiftly shift my energy towards the solution in order to attract positive outcomes. Journaling about this was incredibly powerful, as it allowed me to narrate the story as if it had already unfolded. By writing in the past tense, I was sending a clear message to the universe that I now possess what I desired. This shifted my vibrational energy from focusing on the problem to being in alignment with solutions, circumstances, and situations that led me to my desired outcomes. It's important to recognize that thinking from a place, or focusing on the problem can only generate more problems.

- *I remember... (Neville Goddard)*

This exercise is similar to the one mentioned above. It involves selecting a random date in the future, whether it's a year from now or the end of your lifetime and crafting a story of how you envision things unfolding. For instance:

- *I remember a time when I wasn't a millionaire (programming the energetic assumption that you now are), but then I had this incredible idea that transformed my financial situation. What happened next was truly remarkable...*

- *I remember when I felt exhausted and overwhelmed all the time (programming in the energetic assumption that you no longer are). However, when I made a conscious decision to establish boundaries with my work, everything began to change...*

Both of these exercises are highly effective because they allow you to acknowledge your current circumstances without judgment or negativity. It's simply a snapshot in time. And yet, you don't leave the future to chance. Instead, take control of life and co-create the next chapters with the universe, learning your own life lessons along the way.

By the way, Craig and I rekindled our relationship a few months later, and in that particular month I made more than all the expenses combined (just). Craig and I addressed some of the deeper patterns that were holding us back, and now, two years later, we are stronger than ever. This is the reward you receive when you delve deep into your inner world during moments of chaos, pain, or challenge. No matter how skilled you become at manifesting, life will always present you with opportunities to choose greater awakening or remain stagnant. Interestingly, the more you resist and judge your present circumstances, the more you become stuck in them. However, when you embrace and love every aspect of your journey, including the challenges and perceived failures, you propel yourself to new heights. It's quite fascinating, isn't it?

Over time, your journal will not only serve as a reminder of your growth and the wonderful things that already exist in your life, but also as a powerful tool for self-reflection. It'll help align your subconscious with your goals and guide you as your dreams change or new ones show up. This documentation will prove your progress and support your manifestation journey.

Breathwork for Success

Breathing exercises are helpful for reducing stress because they help calm the nervous system, lower heart rate, and decrease blood pressure. By focusing on controlled breathing, you can shift your attention away from stressors, promoting relaxation and mental clarity. These exercises also increase oxygen flow to the brain, improving mood and reducing anxiety. Regular practice of breathing techniques can enhance overall emotional well-being and resilience to stress.

I also want to note that breathwork is beneficial when you are not stressed. For example, do this when you first wake up or before having a cup of coffee. Take five minutes to do breathing exercises. It can also prepare your mind and body to invite and receive inspired ideas and thoughts.

Here is a quick, simple example of breathwork to reduce stress:

- Sit or lie down in a comfortable position.

- If that feels safe, close your eyes or look down toward your chest.

- Breathe naturally for a few minutes.

- When ready, inhale gently through your nose to fill your belly, ribs and chest.

- Gently exhale through your mouth until you feel empty.

- Inhale again, gently through your nose to your belly.

- Exhale entirely through your mouth, making a whooshing sound, until empty.

- Repeat this cycle 10 more times or until you feel ready.

- Return your breathing to a natural rhythm.

This method helps to calm the mind and body, reducing stress and promoting relaxation.

Raising Your Vibration

Imagine walking into a room and instantly feeling lighter, as if the air is lifting your spirits. This sensation is not just about what you see or hear but about the energy you are stepping into. Every person, place, and object vibrates at a specific frequency, affecting your moods and feelings and your ability to attract what you desire in life. This chapter is dedicated to understanding and enhancing your vibrational energy, which can significantly boost your manifestation efforts.

Definition Of Vibrational Energy

Vibrational energy might sound scientific, but it is something you experience every day. It refers to the frequency at which everything in the universe, including you and me, oscillates. Everything has a vibration, from the chair you are sitting on to the thoughts you think. These vibrations are not static; they change depending on various factors, such as your emotions, physical health, and environment. Emotions like love and joy have higher frequencies, while fear and anger vibrate at lower frequencies.

Understanding that you are not just a physical being, but also a vibrational one opens up new ways to shape your life experiences. By learning to raise your vibration, you can enhance your ability to attract positive experiences and desired outcomes into your life. This is because, according to the Law of Attraction, like attracts like—the energy you emit is the energy you attract.

Tools For Measuring Vibration

Measuring vibrational energy can seem challenging, but several tools and techniques can help. One popular method is kinesiology, often referred to as muscle testing. This technique can test the body's responses to different thoughts and emotions, indicating changes in vibrational energy. Another fascinating tool is aura photography, which uses unique cameras to capture your aura's colors, each representing different vibrational frequencies. These colors can provide insight into your emotional and energetic state.

While these tools are helpful, the most accessible tool is your body and awareness. Paying attention to how you *feel* in different situations, particularly your *emotional responses*, can be an excellent indicator of your vibrational state. Remember your vibrational state is only telling you what radio station you are on, there isn't good or bad, just ask yourself *"What station am I plugged into? Is it giving me the results I want?"*

Feeling light, clear, and energized typically suggests higher vibrations, while feeling heavy, cloudy, and stressed can indicate lower vibrations. Notice that you'll *feel* differently about different things, showing you where you do, and don't have resistance. For example:

- You think about your goal and feel a huge pressure on your chest. Thoughts flood into your mind... *"What if I don't create it? Everyone will think I am a failure."* This shows resistance to the desire, and not (yet) being in alignment with what you want. Anxiety can be a sign of a big blessing trying to come through. To allow it in, you can do some clearing work, as discussed in chapter 4.

- You think about your goal, and feel deeply excited, how it's fun, easy, and light. You don't care when it's coming. You're certain it will...and wow, how magnificent will that be. This vibrational state shows you are in harmony with what you want, so it will come quickly, and easily.

The Correlation Between Vibration And Manifestation

The link between your vibrational state and your ability to manifest your desires is profound. Higher vibrational states enhance your overall well-being and accelerate your manifestation capabilities. When you operate at a higher frequency, you align more closely with the universe's frequency of abundance and success, making it easier to attract what you desire. This doesn't mean you must strive to feel ecstatic all the time—life is a spectrum of experiences—but it does mean that cultivating a generally high vibrational state can significantly improve your ability to manifest effectively.

Take this example from Adrianne, she joined one of my 30 day sales challenges to learn how to put herself out there and make money from her passion. She didn't make any art sales that month as she predicted, but something unexpected happened. She attended a concert she hadn't planned on going to, deciding at the last minute because she received free tickets. She made another last minute decision to drive her car to the concert, and it was so crowded that finding parking took a long time. She eventually parked in a tight space, and after the concert, she discovered that someone had bumped her car, leaving a few scratches. Adrianne received about €1200 from the insurance company for these minor scratches. Additionally, she received another €1200 from her parents without any specific reason.

In simple terms, though Adrianne didn't sell any art that specific month, she still ended up with money coming her way out of the blue. From a law of attraction and manifestation perspective, it's all about the vibration you're putting out. Adrianne was hoping to make money through art sales, but instead, she got it through unexpected means—like insurance for a minor car scratch and a surprise gift from her parents. The key idea here is that the universe found a way to deliver money to her because the frequency was right, even if it wasn't through art. It's proof that when you're in the right mindset and putting out the right energy, things that are a match to your vibration will come to you, often in ways you wouldn't expect.

Enhancing Your Vibrational Energy Through Mindful Practices

One effective way to enhance vibrational energy is through mindful practices promoting relaxation and joy. Meditation, yoga, and time in nature are excellent activities that can help elevate your vibration naturally. When you engage in meditation and intentionally redirect your focus away from the thoughts in your mind, such as by listening to the sound of a lawn mower or the hum of an air conditioner, a remarkable change can occur. By sitting in silence and consciously concentrating on a repetitive noise, you will gradually notice a change within yourself. Your body's vibration naturally increases, providing a valuable tool for alleviating stress and anxiety related to a specific outcome. With consistent practice, this technique becomes easier, and eventually, you may even experience a state of merging into nothingness, also known as the quantum field, as your body's vibration naturally elevates. It's not uncommon to encounter miraculous experiences on the other side of a meditation process.

I recently experienced a remarkable miracle as a result of surrendering and meditating to allow my vibration to naturally rise. We were facing a complex situation with a program we were hosting, where a booking mistake had occurred, and we were at risk of being charged over €2k for unnecessary rooms. Despite spending the entire day trying to rectify the situation and convince the company to make the necessary changes, they remained steadfast in their policy. In an act of acceptance and surrender, I embraced the possibility of having to pay for a group booking we didn't need. I approached the situation with a willingness to accept the worst-case outcome, which eliminated any fear or resistance towards the desired result. Before going to bed, I dedicated an hour to meditating on nothingness, a specific meditation practice I follow. Surprisingly, the next morning, even after a restless night due to illness, I received a message from Tamsin informing me that they had unexpectedly emailed us to inform us that they were releasing the booking. It was truly a miraculous turn of events.

There is a common belief that the best approach to solving a problem is to brainstorm, obsess over the issue, and be consumed by panic and stress. Many individuals become addicted to panic and stress, often due to an unconscious fear that without it, their lives would unravel and their motivation would disappear. However, this belief is entirely **not** true. In reality, surrendering the problem to the universe, merging with the quantum, and allowing your vibration to naturally elevate can be even more effective in finding a solution. It may not always be in your best interest to play the role of "Miss" or "Mr. Fixit" in every situation.

As you explore these tools and insights, remember that raising your vibration is not about achieving a perfect state of continual bliss. Gradually shift your baseline towards more optimistic and lighter energies, and use processes like meditation to raise your vibration instead of getting stuck in fear and stress. This shift does not just enhance your mood—it transforms your ability to attract and manifest the experiences and outcomes you desire in life.

Daily Manifestation Routines For Busy Individuals

The key to successful manifestation isn't about making grand gestures but about adding small, consistent practices into your daily routine. Even short moments can become powerful with intention. Setting up a routine has lots of benefits. It improves your focus, keeping your mental energy aimed at your goals. It also boosts motivation; having a structured routine can help you stay driven even on tough days. Plus, sticking to a daily routine strengthens your commitment to manifestation, making sure your efforts build up over time, increasing your chances of achieving what you want.

For example, while waiting for your morning coffee to brew or before you start your car, take a minute to affirm your intentions for the day. These might include affirmations like, *"Today, I attract abundance and clarity,"* or, *"I am a magnet for positive outcomes."* It is about setting a tone, a vibrational signature you carry throughout your day, aligning with your broader goals.

Tailoring these routines to fit your lifestyle, time constraints, and personal preferences is crucial. Only some people are morning people, capable of an hour-long meditation at dawn. Brief meditation sessions in the evening or short visualization practices during your lunch break may better suit your schedule and energy levels. Similarly, your affirmations should resonate with your personal beliefs and be phrased in an empowering way. If long journaling sessions feel overwhelming, consider bullet journaling, which can be equally effective. The key is to customize these practices so they enrich your life rather than feel like burdens (which by the way is a belief in itself, I regularly tell myself that commitment and routines are light and fun, and so they are).

Morning And Evening Manifestation Rituals

Morning and evening are pivotal times of the day that can significantly influence your manifestation capabilities. In the morning, your mind is like a clean slate, fresh, receptive, and naturally in an alpha brainwave state (otherwise known as hypnosis). Capitalizing on this, you might start by taking a moment to "see" your day going wonderfully, to send love to every room you'll be in, and all the people you'll speak to before you even jump out of bed. Or spend 10 mins listing things you are grateful for—no matter how small—in your head with your eyes closed. Feel the sense of gratitude in your heart and let it spread throughout your body. This doesn't need to be strenuous exercise. Allow yourself to think whatever comes to your mind without judgment. This practice not only builds a positive mindset but also boosts your expectations for good things to happen, setting you on the right vibe for the day ahead.

On the other hand, evenings are perfect for unwinding and preparing your subconscious for the work it does while you sleep. Before bed, try this 15-minute meditation:

1. Sit or lie in a quiet, comfortable place where you won't be disturbed. Dim the lights or use a soft lamp to create a calming environment.

2. Close your eyes and take a few deep breaths. Inhale deeply through your nose, allowing your abdomen to rise, and then exhale slowly through your mouth. Repeat this three times.

3. Starting from your toes, slowly bring awareness to each body part, moving upwards. Notice any tension or discomfort and consciously release it. Relax your feet, legs, hips, abdomen, chest, arms, hands, neck, and head.

4. Focus on Your Breath. Continue to breathe naturally. Pay attention to the rise and fall of your chest or the sensation of air entering and leaving your nostrils. Let your breath be your anchor to the present moment.

5. As you inhale, imagine drawing in calm and peaceful energy. As you exhale, visualize letting go of any stress, worries, or negative experiences from the day. See them dissolving into the air and fading away.

6. Reflect on three things you are grateful for that happened today. They can be small or significant. Feel the sense of gratitude in your heart, and let it fill you with warmth and contentment.

7. Briefly visualize a peaceful and productive tomorrow. See yourself waking up refreshed and moving through your day with ease and positivity.

8. Silently repeat positive affirmations to yourself. Examples include: *"I am at peace with today." "I release all worries and embrace rest." "I am grateful for today's experiences and look forward to tomorrow."*

9. Slowly bring your awareness back to your breath. Take a moment to notice the sensations in your body and the sounds around you.

10. Take one final deep breath in and out, feeling any remaining tension melt away. When you are ready, gently open your eyes.

If you are preparing for sleep, allow yourself to transition gently into your bedtime routine, carrying a sense of peace and relaxation.

Integrating Manifestation Activities During Commutes

For many, the daily commute is a time of stress or mindless routine. However, it also presents a perfect opportunity to enhance your manifestation routine. If you drive, you can listen to affirmations or inspiring talks that resonate with your goals. In the School of Integrative Healing, we have a plethora of visualization and guided processes in our private meditation podcast. Our students consistently listen to our podcasts in the car, utilizing this time to program in new helpful belief systems. For those who use public transportation, you could consider a guided visualization through headphones, picturing your dreams in vivid detail, These practices transform idle time into powerful sessions of intention-setting and alignment. You'll realize quickly how much time you actually do have.

Maintaining consistency and commitment in your routine can be challenging, especially when faced with distractions or low motivation. Setting small, achievable goals can help build and maintain momentum. For example, commit to meditating for five minutes a day and gradually increase the time as you get more comfortable with the practice. Remember, the goal is to manifest with ease. So be sure to seamlessly integrate these activities into your daily routine so that they become as natural and essential as eating or sleeping.

As you continue these practices, you will likely discover that your ability to manifest grows more robust, your focus sharper, and your life increasingly aligned with your deepest desires. This routine is about achieving specific goals and fostering a lifestyle that continuously nurtures your growth and transformation. By setting up and maintaining a personalized manifestation routine, you are working towards transforming your dreams into reality and actively sculpting a more empowered and purposeful version of yourself.

The next chapter will delve into overcoming obstacles in manifestation, providing you with strategies to navigate and transcend the challenges that might arise on your path to achieving your dreams. This upcoming discussion is pivotal to help you thrive in adversity and turn your dreams into reality.

EXERCISE:

1. Write out your goal in the present tense. For Example: I am a 6 figure earner, who creates with fun and ease; I am in a loving relationship with someone who adores me for who I am.

2. Write out the thoughts and beliefs that are a match to this goal.

3. Write out the feelings and frequency that are a match to this goal. Feel into this exercise. Practice running situations through your mind and feeling them through your body.

4. From this new place of BEING write out your DOING. Some helpful questions to ask yourself whilst you do this:

- how does this version of me begin their day?

- how does this version of me introduce myself?

- how does this version of me speak?

- how does this version organize, plan, or schedule my day?

- how does this version of me spend their spare time?

Allow DIVINE INSPIRATION to flow through you. Trust the illogical ideas that come through and do not judge.

Additional Training Available:

Scan the QR Code or enter the link into your browser to access your FREE training. If you already have an account, you can log in using the link that was provided in your welcome email.

https://manifestwitheasebook.com

Overcoming Obstacles And Objections

L earning how to manifest consciously, doesn't mean it will always be perfect, and that there won't be challenges (however remember within every challenge there is a much bigger blessing). As you cultivate your dreams into reality, understanding what not to do can be just as important as knowing what to do. In this chapter, I will cover common pitfalls and barriers to manifestation that I see repeatedly. Some of this may be reminders of what was already shared. However, you often know things intellectually and then forget about them. It is easy to fall back into old patterns and the past self. There is a myth that once you are aligned, you will always be in a perfect state of alignment, and that is not true. Life is all about regulation, returning to your center, alignment, and remembering what you know. This is why in the School of Integrative Healing, I regularly remind you of these concepts, and we practice and get into the energy together.

When you first start on your manifestation journey, the excitement and eagerness is normal. However, it's easy to lose faith, excitement, or belief as soon as something doesn't go to plan. Recognizing why something hasn't worked, or what to do when you are in the "messy middle" of a manifestation is really helpful. In the School of Integrative Healing, we give you a map for the light and the dark times. Here are some common mistakes that you can easily correct:

Going Straight to the *Doing* , And Forgetting About the State of *Being*

To consciously manifest, you need to change your approach to how you engage with the world. Throughout your lives, you have been conditioned to believe that it's only taking action that leads to desired outcomes (living outside-in). When it comes to building a business, the typical human response is to immerse yourself in relentless activity in the hope of success, especially when driven by fear. If things don't seem to be working, the instinct is to work even harder until exhaustion and resentment set in. Similarly, in relationships, people often find themselves repeating the same patterns, moving from one relationship to another, never pausing, just hoping the next one will be the "one".

Conscious manifestation requires you to embrace the power of pause. Before diving headfirst into a new relationship, it's important to take a moment to reflect and ask yourself crucial questions. Are there any unresolved issues or patterns from past relationships that need healing and clearing? Similarly, in business, when things aren't going well, it's beneficial to pause and inquire, *"What within me is a match to this situation?"* This pause shouldn't be mistaken for inertia, as you create through momentum and consistent action. The pause can be integrated into your daily routine, such as a morning ritual or dedicating time on Friday afternoons to cleanse and declutter your system instead of relentlessly pursuing the next goal. Additionally, pausing for just a few seconds before entering a room allows you to tap into your inner confidence and contemplate how a confident being would carry themselves. A 2-second pause can break negative patterns and give you the choice to engage or not. It breaks the habit and opens up new possibilities.

Remember that you've spent a significant portion of your life allowing external factors to dictate your mood, what you believe is possible, and even your destiny. I'm encouraging you to shift your focus inward and prioritize your inner world while shaping your external reality. It may take time for this new mindset to become second nature, but in the meantime, be patient with yourself. Personal growth entails embracing and accepting who you are, rather than adding more tasks to an endless checklist in order to feel worthy or lovable. So, be mindful of that as well. Remember, you're amazing, even when you make mistakes.

Inconsistency In Practice

Manifestation is not a one-time activity. Consciously manifesting requires consistent practice and dedication. The initial excitement of starting a new manifestation diary or visualization practice can fade after a few days or weeks, especially if immediate results are not seen. Therefore, it is paramount to consistently maintain your conscious manifestation efforts, integrating these practices into your daily life until they become habitual. Consistency yields desired results through daily affirmations, journaling, or meditation. Start with small goals and gradually make each one slightly bigger than the last. This way, you'll have lots of achievements to celebrate, which will help you build self-confidence, rather than setting huge goals that might reinforce the belief that you can't succeed or that the process doesn't work.

Additionally, use reminders or schedule specific times for your manifestation activities to ensure they become an integral part of your daily routine.

Being Impatient And Slowing Down Manifestation

Let's bring it back to day one when I discussed life being a mirror of your inner world. When they start doing manifestation work and changing their beliefs, most people become impatient if life hasn't caught up yet. The dominant thought when you are impatient is like being continually in a scarcity mindset. It's not just about time scarcity, like wondering when it will happen; it can also involve self-criticism and doubt, with thoughts like *"Why is this not working out for me?"* They often throw up their arms and declare that manifestation doesn't work, or it doesn't work for them (yes the universe picked you out, to be the **ONE** person on planet Earth the laws don't apply too). When you feel impatient, you're affirming that it is not here. Your dominant thought is that the thing you desire is not here. What did you already learn? Your inner world creates your outer world. The energy that ripples out will be more of it not being here. Even if you are doing all the work if every day you are thinking it is not here, that *"it's not here"* will be your radio station of choice and will...lead to it not being here. Just this can slow you down, but no biggie, there's no rush anyway. This is why one of my affirmations is *"There's so much time to be, do, and have everything I want"*.

What does patience represent? Patience represents trust and faith. Patience represents energetically being in the goal. Patience speeds up manifestation. What I remember most about my biggest quantum leaps in finances or love, is that I was very relaxed. I got myself out of the way and trusted that the universe was with me every single step of the way. If you're busy clutching and gripping, not only is your physical body going through stress and tension, but your energy and vibration are locked into wanting to take control (lack of trust), so the energy of the thing you desire comes slower. And not a big deal, because you can change today.

Forgetting There Is A Gestation Period

Many people overlook the gestation period inherent in conscious manifestation. Consider pregnancy: it's not simply the moment sperm meets egg, and then the baby arrives instantly. Imagine the chaos that would ensue without the nine months of preparation mentally and emotionally for the baby's arrival. Nature demonstrates the universal laws through this process. Similarly, when you manifest, there's a gestation period between having the desire and its fulfillment. This period is the natural process in which things are created, though, unlike pregnancy, its duration is unpredictable.

Impatience often causes people to start inner work, see no immediate change, and then give up, reverting to thoughts of lack instead of staying focused on their goals. Look at King Richard (go watch the film, I promise you won't regret it). One of the fascinating things about Richard (the Williams sisters' dad) was that he wrote their tennis success plan before the girls were born and patiently put it into action for 15 years until Venus signed her first $12 million deal in 1995. Talk about the long game. His plan for Venus has won her 49 singles titles over her career, and Serena 73, so it's fair to say that extra inch of patience worked wonders. Patience accelerates manifestation. Because patience represents trust, and certainty in the desirable outcome, and if you are sure, what's the rush? Have fun on the way, baby.

You Are Telling The Wrong Story

Everything happening in your life is inherently neutral. They're just facts. Your creative power lies in the narratives you tell about your experiences, which makes you feel emotions (thoughts lead to feelings). For example, and this is a big and poignant example, the neutral facts are: when I was 19 my mum was diagnosed with cancer for the first time. By the time I was 23, it was terminal, and three years later she passed away on July 16th, 2019. When I share these facts, 99% of people will say, *"I'm so sorry, that must have been terrible"*. While there's truth in their response, I have refused since my early 20s to accept their view as my reality or the story I tell. I refuse to see my life as a tragedy. I think of my life as a story of overcoming, of triumph, of love and possibility.

Around 24 or 25, I realized that my internal perspective dictated everything in my life. So, instead of telling myself *"My mum is dying, this is terrible, life is shit, and why do bad things happen to me"*, I started telling myself *"My mum is dying, and this is the best thing that has ever happened to me."* It sounds wild, right? How can my mum's death be the best thing that has ever happened to me? How can being in and out of palliative care for three years in my 20s be good? I'll tell you, and I cannot say it enough, watching my mum die taught me how to live. Her death and everything surrounding it was the most magnificent and life-altering thing to happen to me. But I could only see it that way because of the story I chose to tell myself. I told myself again and again that this was good. So again, and again I kept seeing the good. Then the good kept amplifying, and my life kept getting better and better.

What is true? Is "life bad" or is "this the best thing to ever happen to me?" You choose. You CHOOSE. YOU CHOOSE! That's your power. You get to decide every moment whether this is the "worst thing ever" or the "best thing ever." Everything in your life depends on what you focus on and the story you tell yourself. That's how powerful you are.

Just to be clear, I'm not saying I didn't grieve. I grieved deeply. But now, five years later, I can honestly say, with a hand to my heart, that when I think of my mum, all I can do is smile and be truly grateful for the 26 years I shared with her. It wasn't too much or too little, but just the perfect amount. And the love? It's infinite.

The Influence Of The People And Environment On Your Energy

Your environment and the people around you have a big impact on your vibrational energy. Your daily surroundings and social interactions can either *nourish* you with positive energy or *drain you*. Everything around you—from your physical space to your social circle—affects the vibe you're in, which influences your mood, thoughts, and ability to manifest your desires effectively.

In his book *The Biology of Belief*, Dr. Bruce Lipton states that 60% of your beliefs are programmed before the age of six. Sometimes, you manifest things and question which part of you created those things. Your conscious mind would have never created them. You may be unaware of your beliefs because they are not yours—they are your parents', your environment's, and your early surroundings.' The belief work is inner child work. It is reprogramming the beliefs from your early environment. As an adult, you can program new beliefs through repeated thought, or other healing processes. When a thought becomes a belief, it impacts your biology and your life. Imagine you keep telling yourself, *"I'm terrible at public speaking."* At first, it's just a thought. But if you keep thinking it, you start to believe it. This belief makes you feel super anxious whenever you have to speak in front of others. Your heart races, you sweat, and you might even stumble over your words. This anxiety can then lead to avoiding public speaking altogether, which affects your career or social life. That simple thought turned belief actually changes how your body reacts and impacts your life in a big way.

It's when a thought becomes a belief that creation becomes effortless. Another personal example, right now, my belief is not to make six figures in a year; my unconscious programming is to make more. With that belief cemented now, it would be more difficult for me to make 6-figures a year (my old program) than to make more (my new program).

The people you choose to surround yourself with can have an equally profound impact on your vibrational state. A constantly complaining person in your circle can impact the collective energy, affecting everyone's mood and vibrational frequency. It can lead to everyone suddenly having more to complain about (what you focus on grows). On the flip side, being around people who are positive, supportive, and aligned with your values can significantly uplift your spirits, and belief in what's possible for you and boost your energy. Therefore, it is essential to be mindful of the energy you allow into your life from social interactions, choosing to spend time with those who reflect the kind of energy you want to embody and attract. Joining containers or communities with coaches and other like-minded individuals can be transformational because you are putting yourself into an environment that is congruent with your dreams.

Dealing With Doubt: How To Keep Faith When Results Are Not Visible

There is a tendency to judge certain emotions as "wrong." When feelings of frustration, doubt, stress, or impatience arise, they don't feel good, so the immediate impulse is often to change them. Doubt can dampen your spirits and cloud your vision, especially when the tangible outcomes of your manifestation efforts are not immediately visible. It's natural to experience doubt; your human brain is wired to seek evidence and reassurance. However, sometimes it's valuable to allow yourself to sit with and experience the emotion fully for a day. You're allowed a day in bed to be grumpy. Remember my story of the €100k bill, and how I gave myself the opportunity for a pity party first? Letting your emotions flow naturally, without fighting them, can help you feel better pretty quickly. If this shift doesn't happen, it may indicate there is inner healing work to be addressed.

Here is an empowering thought: doubt is not necessarily a blockade. Instead, it can serve as a tool for deeper self-awareness and commitment. When doubt creeps in, it challenges you to reassess your beliefs and the strength of your convictions, pushing you to reinforce your mental and emotional foundations.

What if you viewed your emotions not as problems to be fixed but as valuable information to explore your inner realms? The next time you find yourself in a situation overwhelmed with undesirable feelings, grab a piece of paper and write down everything you're thinking that is creating the undesirable feelings, then apply Byron Katie's four questions from her book *Loving What Is*:

- Is it true?

- Can you absolutely know that it's true? *(the answer here is always no)*

- How do you react when you believe that thought?

- Who would you be without the thought?

By engaging with these questions, you unravel the stories you tell yourself about a situation. You'll see that nine out of ten times it's the stories causing the emotional pain, not what is actually happening (remember everything is neutral, you add the story). The goal is to examine your thoughts, see if they are helpful, and imagine how you might feel without them. The simple energetic shift from story to another possibility can lead to pretty radical changes.

Recently, a client approached me for help navigating a challenging situation involving money, she was in a bit of a sticky situation. I encouraged her to use these four questions. The next day, she unexpectedly received a raise at work, and not only was she able to pay the unexpected bills, but she now had a permanent increase in income. Fun. The universe is abundant, and countless solutions and opportunities can flow into your life by releasing limiting beliefs and changing your point of attraction. Sometimes, you even experience what can be described as instant manifestations.

Consider this perspective: What if your doubt serves as the catalyst for strengthening your faith? Take a moment to engage with your doubts and explore them using Byron Katie's four questions. Once you've done this, reflect on how you feel.

Additionally, one of the simplest methods to enhance your faith is by surrounding yourself with individuals who possess a strong belief in possibility. Belief systems and energy have a magic quality—they have the ability to transfer to those around them, including yourself.

The Impact Of Past Traumas On Current Manifestation Efforts

When you are working hard to manifest your dreams, it can sometimes feel like an unseen force is holding you back. Often elusive and deeply buried, this barrier could be rooted in past traumas. Unresolved traumas can subconsciously influence your current manifestation efforts, creating blocks that might prevent you from achieving desired outcomes. Note, that you don't need to be perfect to manifest because you're always manifesting. But if you keep getting the same unwanted results or it's been a real struggle to reach a goal, it might mean there's some deep-rooted trauma needing to be cleared. It's like trying to sail a boat still anchored; no matter how much wind fills your sails, you will not move forward until you lift that anchor. Traumas, whether big or small, can anchor your energy in past fears and doubts, affecting how you perceive and interact with the world today.

Manifestation cannot be discussed without talking about healing trauma and past experiences from your outer environment. One way to heal from past experiences is known as inner child healing. In the School of Integrative Healing, we use a trauma-informed approach to manifestation, which is unusual but necessary. Understanding the link between past traumas and manifestation blocks is vital. Traumatic experiences imprint on your subconscious, shaping your beliefs and frequency. For instance, if you have ever experienced an expansion of finances that came with a lot of criticism and rejection, you might subconsciously develop a fear that any money you manifest will come with pain, so you subtly sabotage more coming in. Similarly, experiences of rejection or failure might instill a fear of trying new opportunities or limiting your potential to manifest new experiences.

Healing from trauma is not just beneficial for your well-being but extremely helpful for effective manifestation. Integrating professional help is often necessary when dealing with deep-seated traumas. While self-help techniques can offer significant benefits, professional coaches or therapists can provide the expertise and support needed to navigate through complex emotional landscapes. They can help you uncover hidden traumas you might not even be aware of and offer tools and strategies for long-term healing and recovery, which is what we do in the School of Integrative Healing in a group setting. Healing is about gathering a variety of tools to make sure your path to your dreams is clear and smooth and having the right tools for different situations.

Kamilla came to me seeking guidance to improve her money goals. What I didn't realize at the time was she had been in a 13-year-long battle with chronic anxiety. She had suffered from anywhere between 1000-3000 anxiety attacks in her lifetime. Her body was carrying such intense trauma...After four months of no meds, only focusing on emotional clearing techniques, like the shamanic techniques, and belief work she stopped having these attacks. A year later she sent a beautiful message with an update that she was still 'anxiety free', something she doesn't declare lightly, and was feeling happier than ever before.

Handling External Skepticism And Negative Feedback

When you are a big dreamer, encountering skepticism and negative feedback, especially from those close to you, can seem inevitable. It is essential to remember that such reactions are often more about the other person's beliefs and fears than about you or your manifestation abilities. Strengthening your conviction in your manifestation practice is about lovingly ignoring these external voices and reinforcing your internal dialogue with positivity and faith.

This is a story of how holding your faith and living your life by example is the best solution to overcoming skepticism. A client shared how both she and her husband were informed that they were receiving extra paychecks one year, just before New Year. These came out of nowhere and there was no special reason for them. They work at different companies and her husband had worked for his company for 10 years and had never once received any kind of Christmas or New Year's bonus. She said he never doubted manifestation again after that.

Here's another fun story about holding the faith despite what your partner thinks. A client had been declaring to her partner for two weeks straight that they would manifest $1000 selling their goods at their first market. He refused to believe her as in previous weeks they had only sold $50-$100 per week on average. What do you think they made at their first market? $1000.

Strengthening Personal Conviction

To stand firm in your beliefs despite skepticism, deepening your understanding and connection to the manifestation process is essential. Educate yourself about the principles of manifestation, not just as a practice but as a lifestyle, immersing yourself in literature, videos, and workshops that reinforce your understanding and commitment. The more knowledge you have, the more confident you will feel in your practice. Additionally, keep up with your success journals. As you see more evidence of manifestation happening in your own life, your belief will become stronger, leading to more manifestations. It is an ideal circle to be in. Continue reaffirming your daily commitment through small rituals or affirmations that align with your goals. These practices are constant reminders of your journey's purpose and the reasons behind your choice to adopt conscious manifestation as a part of your life.

Transforming Criticism Into Constructive Feedback

Criticism can be a valuable tool if you can distinguish between negativity that aims to tear down and criticism that aims to build up. When you receive feedback, take a moment to assess its intent and content. Ask yourself whether there is a kernel of truth or a lesson to be learned that can refine your manifestation practices. For example, if your goal is a relationship, are you attracting non-committal partners because deep down you don't believe anyone would want to love you? Maybe there's an aspect to your approach you haven't considered, or more importantly, remember that your external world is feedback to your internal world. If people keep saying the same thing to you, instead of being mad, reflect, is this something I am secretly telling myself? Therefore, criticism is a chance to see what your external world says about your subconscious. Use this as an opportunity for growth, applying what is useful and discarding what is not. This approach enhances your manifestation skills and contributes to your personal development.

Handling external skepticism and negative feedback requires a blend of self-confidence, protective strategies, open communication, and discernment. By strengthening your belief in your personal path, shielding yourself from unwarranted negativity, managing relationships with care, and turning criticism into opportunities for growth, you empower yourself to continue your manifestation journey with resilience and joy. These strategies ensure that your path remains clear and focused, driven by your inner vision, and shielded from external doubts and negativity. As you implement these practices, you will find that your ability to manifest your desires becomes more robust and more aligned with your true self, unaffected by what others think.

The Messy Middle

Before experiencing a significant transformation that requires substantial inner change, there is often a period known as the *"messy middle."* During this time, you're no longer the person you used to be, but you haven't fully become who you're meant to be either. It can be an incredibly uncomfortable phase where many individuals are tempted to revert to what is familiar and known due to the discomfort of the present moment. However, by doing so, they miss out on their dreams, which is on the other side of the discomfort. This is why it's important to acknowledge and normalize the *"messy middle"* - a chunk of time where it may seem like everything is falling apart, even though it may actually be falling into place. The only way to navigate through this phase is to keep moving forward, nurture your desires, and maintain faith in the process.

Here's a great example: After staying for what she described as 5 long years, Tamsin decided it was time to leave her unhealthy relationship. She couldn't tolerate her partner's unsupportive behavior any longer. However, leaving the relationship came with its own challenges. Leaving the relationship meant also leaving the house and having to look for a new home. It meant facing being alone and confronting her inner demons. It felt like a lot at once. Tamsin found herself deep in the messy middle where everything appeared to have fallen apart. Instead of reverting to her old ways, she was committed to doing the inner work necessary to move forward. For a year Tamsin focused on dismantling her limiting beliefs, like peeling back the layers of an onion. She was dedicated to creating a new self-image that was a match with the partner she desired. A few months ago, she met the perfect man, that matched everything she had been seeking, at the TV station where I had a segment in Marbella. This would not have been possible if she had returned to her old partner, home, and life whenever she felt sad, anxious, or lonely. It's wonderful to talk about the things you can manifest, but it's also important to remember that to receive some of those things, you must be willing to let go of the old and create space for the new to enter your life.

If you're in the messy middle but are determined to push through to the other side, you have what it takes to truly change your life. I've often considered retreating to the familiar in various aspects of my life—business, love, location—but to manifest the life you desire, it's not just about affirmations. You have to be brave and do the things most people don't.

As I wrap up this exploration of overcoming obstacles in manifestation, remember that each challenge is an opportunity for growth and self-discovery. Whether navigating doubts, dealing with external skepticism, or confronting internal fears, the strategies discussed here are designed to empower you and enhance your journey toward manifesting your dreams.

Your homework for today is to rewrite a story in your life that has been holding you back. For example, your story could be about debt or not being where you want to be financially. Maybe you think, *"I'm not where I wanted to be at my age."* I hear that all the time. By writing down these stories, you cultivate awareness of the inner narrative that is blocking you. Remember to forgive yourself for having them. You are human and you will pick up stories, which is fine. But now you have to start rewriting them to consciously change them.

My partner Craig, whom I lovingly call "the bagel," used to always say, *"Everything in my life is going well, except for finances."* He repeated it to me constantly, until one day I said *"yes, darling it will stay this way as long as you keep saying this."* Three years later and I can say that statement is absolutely not true in any way. Remember, whatever story you tell yourself will be reflected in your daily life.

EXERCISE:

- Pick something in your life that isn't working.

- Write a brain dump on the page (just write, don't judge)

- Separate everything you have written into facts and stories:

  - Facts (what cannot be disputed, for example, my name is Jana)

  - Stories (everything you have bound around the facts)

- Identify the stories that have not been helpful

- Rewrite these stories using the "I remember..." exercise from chapter 3.

  - Example: I remember when I used to think I was fat and old every time I looked in the mirror. Then I started to notice the beauty I was missing—the sparkle in my eyes and the grace in how I moved. I began eating in a way that showed love to my body and started going to dance classes. Within a year, I hardly recognized the woman in the mirror. The confidence, love, and certainty were clear

- Read the new story every morning until it becomes real.

The exercise is not just about being aware of the stories you tell yourself that hold you back. When you rewrite your story, you are reclaiming your power and reminding yourself that you are the author of your life. It shifts your focus from limitations to possibilities, fostering a mindset of abundance and success. This exercise helps reprogram limiting beliefs and aligns your thoughts with what you truly desire, enhancing clarity and motivation. By envisioning and narrating your story from a place of achievement, you empower yourself to take proactive steps toward manifesting your desired outcomes with confidence and determination.

Additional Training Available:

Here is today's FREE training. Scan the QR Code or enter the link into your browser to access your bonus training. If you already have an account you can log in using the link that was provided in your welcome email.

https://manifestwitheasebook.com

Common Questions, Success Stories, And The Future

I magine flipping through the pages of your own life story, where each chapter is filled with moments of triumph, insights, and substantial growth. This part of the book is just like that—a collection of inspiring tales where real people, much like yourself, have turned their financial tides from overwhelming debts to abundant prosperity, or taken themselves from chronic pain to freedom of mobility because manifestation can be applied to anything. These people accomplished all of these feats using the principles of manifestation. These stories are not just narratives; they are proof of the potent power within you to transform your reality.

I will begin by answering some of the questions that were asked during one of my workshops so you can get a feeling of what other people were thinking and feeling too around this topic.

What If I Do Not Know What I Want?

Let's start here. Instead of waking up and focusing on everything you have to do and your commitments, which can create undesirable feelings or pressure, say to yourself, *"I am going to find what I enjoy today and seek clarity."* You find clarity through experience. Listen to life and you'll start seeing what you enjoy and want more of, and also what you don't enjoy, that you want less of. This is a form of clarity.

However, what happens if you keep affirming to yourself, *"I do not have clarity,"* or *"I do not know what I want?"* You may even feel shame for not having more clarity, pushing clarity even further away. From what you have learned in this book, what does this do? It creates more "not having clarity." So start by saying to yourself, *"I am creating clarity."* Tell yourself, *"Today, my purpose is to be open to clarity, and to find what feels good, what I like"* Start with that basic approach, and trust that this will guide you towards what you want.

At the end of your day, write down what you enjoyed today. This second step will help you identify what you like and bring you closer to finding clarity. In this process, you learn more about yourself as you experience life. However, be careful to avoid holding onto the story that you are lost or stuck. This is just a story, not a truth. You cannot be lost and stuck because life is forever flowing. "Stuck" and "lost" are just narratives that can be changed and are not facts. So stop telling yourself that, or you will attract more "stuckness" into your life.

People think I went from 0 to success with full clarity. But I think it's important to stress that I spent a good 3-4 years after university traveling and figuring out what I wanted. It wasn't until my mum was in her final year that I even considered starting a business. You see your experiences have a funny way of pushing you towards things you may not have contemplated. You are exactly where you're meant to be.

How Do I Not Feel Like A Fake?

How do I implement this new way of thinking without it feeling fake or that I am just trying to convince myself that I can do this?

The feeling of fakeness or trying to convince yourself often arises when what you desire feels too much of a stretch, unattainable, or impossible (it's not, it's just unpracticed). In these cases, you can use what is called a bridging thought. Remember, the goal is not the thing itself—it is not the money, the house, the lover, or whatever you desire. Choosing something that feels big takes you on a beautiful, powerful journey of self-awareness and growth. It is this journey that is ultimately the goal. Understanding this helps to alleviate some of the fear, because if the journey is the goal, then you can't lose.

For example, if you want to be a multi-millionaire and that feels too far-fetched, you can choose bridging thoughts like *"I could become a multi-millionaire"* or *"I am opening myself to the possibility that I could be a multi-millionaire."* You might also think, *"If I were a multi-millionaire, I would feel..."* This is a lighter approach, playful, without the need. Another example of playing in possibility could look like, *"I could meet my soulmate today"* or *"How would I feel if I met the woman for me today"* Because you are playing with it gently, and NOT needing it to happen today to feel good, or judging the desire, then it's easier for it to come through. This is a lighter way to work with affirmations when you are feeling "fake" or resistant.

Note, that you ultimately want to work towards a solid "*I am*" statement rather than an "*I will or I would*" statement. Saying "*I will*" in the energetic world is equivalent to saying "*I am not.*" For example, "*I will earn 30k per month.*" In the quantum energetic sphere, there is no such thing as time, so "*I will*" keeps you in an energy of longing and not having. Many of our bodies are used to being in longing and desiring to the point that it becomes more comfortable than having. This is why you may feel fake.

When you start with affirmations and new thought patterns, they might not feel authentic at the beginning. But the more you work with them, the more comfortable you become with them. When I first started saying "*I'm financially abundant*", I felt embarrassed. At the time I was living in a shared flat barely able to pay my portion of the rent. I judged myself, thinking it was outrageous and asking, "*Who am I to even want that?*" I turned that around and started thinking it was fantastic that I had those feelings because they helped me explore their origin. My dad is not impressed by money, so naturally, I had internalized some of his beliefs, and even felt shame at my desire. I used those feelings as an opportunity to do the healing work around my limitations regarding my wants. The more I cleared that, the more comfortable I became holding more and more money, allowing for bigger, and better experiences. Not bad for the hippy chick with a big dream.

I Am Waiting To Hear Back About A Job. Do I Keep Trying To Manifest It?

I went to a job interview and am still waiting for their reply. Do I continue to manifest the job or look into other opportunities?

Does it have to be that job, or can it be any other job? Here is another question: Are you thinking from your goal (having a job) or your current state (no job)? This is key. Let's say two people are in the same situation: You and person number two. You had the interview, and you have yet to hear back. Your thought goes to, "*I didn't get the job,*" which is thinking from your present state of lack, not from the being of the goal.

The other person attended the interview and has yet to hear back. Still, this person has a belief system that says, "*It's so easy to get a job.*" So their thinking might be, "*I haven't heard back because many people were interviewing,*" or "*Cool, it's just one job of many. I'm sure I will get another opportunity.*" How can you get yourself into the certainty that you'll get a job, and that there's nothing to fear because a job is on the horizon? You may have to clear some belief systems, like "*it's hard to get a job*" or "*people don't see me and always pick someone else*", that's the real work.

What If I Do Not Believe I Am Powerful Enough?

Where is the belief that you must be powerful? You don't need to be powerful to manifest. As a human being, you manifest simply because you are alive. Everyone can manifest. Sometimes, when you hold limiting beliefs about your power and worth, it helps to examine these utilizing the exercises I have taught in this book. This is also why keeping a journal of your successes is valuable, as it helps you build belief in **YOURSELF.** But, as for manifestation, it's a universal law, a science. You don't need to be powerful to be a creator. You just need to apply the process.

How Do I Know What Beliefs I Have?

Your life reveals all the answers. Examine your life and what you are experiencing. Brain dump everything in your life that isn't going your way, then underline all the unhelpful stories you are telling yourself. Remember, the feedback loop. If you are experiencing something that doesn't feel good, trace it back to the thought and the story you are telling yourself. Your life reflects your thoughts, feelings, and beliefs. If something is happening in your life that you don't like, ask yourself: What part of my past created that? What part of my belief created that? Then, begin to change it. Be the scientist of your life, let it be fun.

Also, note there are a multitude of other modalities that directly track what is in the unconscious. There isn't enough space for all of this in this book, but this is what we teach in the School of Integrative Healing.

Manifesting Goals: Taking Responsibility For Our Lives

I want you to understand that you possess limitless potential on an energetic level, and your task is to expand into that potential in every aspect of your life. As I mentioned earlier, the prerequisite for this work is taking 100% responsibility—especially when it's challenging. This approach accelerates tremendous personal growth.

A few years ago, I joined a business community, and everyone was astonished because I went through a huge financial quantum leap. It was rapid, exponential growth. Many others in the same community did not achieve similar results, prompting questions about what I was doing differently.

The answer lies in my commitment to taking full responsibility for everything that manifests in my life, especially when it's uncomfortable. My life is a reflection of my thoughts and energy. Anything that manifests in my life, I must be consciously or unconsciously contributing to its creation. So, when something appears in my life or business that I don't desire, my first question is: What past thoughts, feelings, and actions led to this manifestation? It's a universal law that applies to everyone, including myself. I then take proactive steps to clear and transform these thoughts into ones that align with my goals.

My client Daniella explains how taking responsibility for her own life allowed her to leave her undesirable job and become a digital nomad traveling the world freely.

> *"For me, joining the school was a pivotal moment where I couldn't return to where I was. I had to move forward. It was a significant quantum leap, and TSIH held me in tough times. While I was at the TSIH, I left a job in marketing that I wasn't in alignment with, but continued to show up for work no matter what; I found a dream job at the time that allowed me to travel the world making €4,000 a month from a couple of months of no income.*

> *This was the first time I started to notice the magick of this work. I always come back to this work over and over again. What I'm constantly reminded of in this work is the importance of self-responsibility. I've learned I've got to show up with presence and unconditional love*

for the inner work. It's my reality that I create what I desire to become, from learning the laws of the universe to understanding actually what surrendering means to becoming an embodied empowered creator.

Not only does magick happen over time, but the more you do this work, the faster it happens because you're constantly letting go of what doesn't serve you. The more we do the work, the 'faster' we start to see the shifts as more of our frequencies begin to resonate with that of the universe, which is who we are in our eternity.

For example, within six days, after I did one simple reprogramming technique with Jana, I went from feeling lack in a particular energetic pattern regarding money to feeling more open in my radiance to the universe. After this, I was gifted money, rent, and other incredible opportunities that have been kept confidential for the time being. The more we do the work, the more we vibrate true nature which is naturally magnetic. The wealth of the universe shows up in mysterious ways, and it always amazes me each time. "

Manifesting Health: Overcoming Chronic Illness With Mindset Shifts

When addressing health challenges, the stories often unheard of are those where individuals tap into their inner strength and, through a deep connection between mind and body, achieve remarkable recoveries or significantly enhance their quality of life. These narratives go beyond medical treatments, focusing on healing techniques that highlight the powerful link between mental state and physical health.

There couldn't be a more remarkable health journey than Tamsin's story. When Tamsin was eight, she was diagnosed with Ulcerative Colitis (UC). It took a year for doctors to figure it out because, 35 years ago, no one thought kids could have it. Once diagnosed, she was put on harsh steroids and other meds to ease the pain, reduce inflammation, and calm her nervous system. Imagine being a kid and having to take all that! Her condition was so severe they decided to remove her entire large intestine replacing it with a piece of her small intestine. The 14-hour-long surgery was full of complications, I would call it the worst in medical history on how not to do surgery. Over the next few years, Tamsin had seven more emergency surgeries.

Tamsin repeatedly heard doctors and family say she would live a 'limited' life and should expect to be on meds forever. Her hospital visits continued for over 30 years, even her 30th birthday was spent in the hospital. The entire experience was too much, it filled her with a lot of shame, guilt, and trauma. Between the ages of 30 and 38, hospital visits became an annual thing due to the build-up of inflammation and internal scar tissue caused by each surgery. Each hospital stay lasted one to two weeks with intravenous morphine, antibiotics, and food, followed by a two to three week recovery before she could go back to work.

Fast forward to five years ago. Tamsin was in the hospital again and this time, she declared she was done with this life. She made a decision that she wanted anything but hospital visits and from there, her healing journey began. Six months later, she discovered ANF Therapy®, a non-invasive, needle-free, and chemical-free way to reduce pain and swelling. It was a dream come true for Tamsin, providing her with much-needed emotional support and becoming her safe place.

Another six months later, she met me. She was searching for new opportunities in work and health, and that's when I introduced her to my idea of The School of Integrative Healing. She dove right in, fully committed to the inner work, attending all the classes, and applying what she learned. She learned about the nervous system, the impact of stress, and how to manage it. She explored shamanic practices, which quickly became her favorite. She was dedicated to creating a new life for herself, knowing that the alternative was ending up back in the hospital, which wasn't an option.

Now, Tamsin has been out of the hospital for over five years. She has a romantic relationship she loves, a beautiful flat in a mountain village in Spain, walks her dog every day, and works out daily. She even does pilates four times a week, something the doctors said she would never be able to do again. And watch out—if you ask her about weekend plans, she might suggest something wild like tree-top climbing or skydiving!

Attracting Love: Real-Life Story Of Manifested Relationships

The quest for love is as old as time. Yet, for many, it feels like a labyrinth where each turn comes with its own challenges—loneliness, the residues of past heartaches, or a repetitive pattern of attracting the wrong kind of partners. These are common themes many individuals face before they find true partnerships. It is not just about finding someone but about having the tools to cultivate long-lasting healthy love (if desired). Manifestation techniques tailored for attracting love focus on drawing the right person into your life and healing and preparing your heart to receive and give love.

For those wanting to attract love, the key takeaway is the importance of you doing the inner work. Being clear about your current state beliefs, and inner world is vital, if not you will keep attracting the same patterns that you don't want. It is also essential to be clear about what you want in a partner and a relationship because remember you aren't chosen, but get to do the choosing. As you reflect on these things, remember that manifesting love is a beautiful blend of knowing what you want, making sure that you are a match, and being open to receiving it. The universe does not just respond to your desires; it responds to your openness.

No one exemplifies this journey better than Kim, who shares her transformative experience in her own words:

> *I hit 48 this year. I've been in two long-term relationships, both turned into marriages. The first one lasted 9 years, and the second one has been 15 amazing years so far. Before all*

COMMON QUESTIONS, SUCCESS STORIES, AND THE...

COMMON QUESTIONS, SUCCESS STORIES, AND THE... 101

this, I had no clue about relationships. I was super depressed and had a lot of inner work to do. Looking back now, I realize I wasn't ready for a relationship then. But back in the day, I was desperate for love, someone to hold me and care about me. I now understand that I needed to love and care for myself first before finding my dream relationship.

I used to hit the clubs and do online dating, trying to meet people. I went on a few dates and had a couple of short-term relationships that lasted up to 6 months, but they all ended badly for me. I was always the one getting dumped, which left me devastated every time. There were so many moments of crying and begging God to help me find someone who loved me for who I was. It took hitting rock bottom for me to finally say, "I GIVE UP!!!" to God. I'm not religious, but I had nowhere else to turn. I completely surrendered, meaning I stopped fighting for what I wanted and decided to open myself up to whatever came my way—whether it was one-night stands, threesomes, short-term dating, or long-term relationships. I didn't care anymore. I did this twice, once before my 9-year relationship and once after it ended. Both times, within a month or two, I found the relationship I desired without having to put myself out there beyond my comfort level.

The first time I surrendered, I had no idea about the law of attraction or manifestation. The second time, I did.

The point is, each time I relinquished control, I shifted my energy from desperation and self-loathing to calm and openness. I worked on my self-confidence and self-love. I stopped judging myself so harshly and started caring for myself more. When I did this the first time, I met my first wife within two months. We were together for nine years. We loved each other, but for two years we fought to stay together. We finally realized that love wasn't enough and decided to divorce because we were just too different.

By the end of this relationship, I was in a much healthier state of mind, thanks to my understanding of the law of attraction and personal development. So, I wrote down on a sticky note all the traits I wanted in my next partner: fun, funny, extroverted, loves traveling, understands manifestation, and is interested in studying it like me. My previous partner didn't have many of these traits, which made us incompatible. I put that note aside, trusting the universe would take care of it. Within a month, I met my current partner. She moved from a different city in a different province, and we met just days after her move. We've been inseparable ever since."

Manifesting Life Transitions: Stories Of Personal Reinvention

In the School of Integrative Healing it's quite normal for people to share significant shifts they experienced after joining the school—like changing careers, moving to a new city, or undergoing deep personal transformations. These transitions aren't just about changing your surroundings—they're all about your inner growth and desires wanting to come out. For a lot of people, these changes start with a feeling that they need something different or more fulfilling, whether it's in their job, where they live, or how they feel inside.

Rachel shares her story of listening to her intuition and body telling her that her current physical body was no longer a match to her authentic self-image. She wanted a chance to reinvent herself. But first, she needed to manifest the means before she could make the physical transition that she desired:

> "I do remember very clearly one day sitting on my sofa and suddenly realizing that after 20 years with breast implants I was fully ready to have them removed from my body. And it was one of those moments as though I'd always known and it was a surprise that I hadn't realized up until that point how much it didn't resonate with me, and it never really resonated with me to have implants in my body. and it was as though all of the pieces of the puzzle had fallen into place. I was so ready and excited to have them out.

I decided at that moment that I was going to have them removed the following winter when I could rest and not be exposed to the sun and the heat and the healing. It didn't really make sense with the business that I was building and the money that was available, to have it done so soon. Yet I decided that it was going to happen and it was really clear, it was a feeling in my body. So the date for booking the operation and having the funds available was getting closer and closer and it was also coinciding with the date for renewing my membership in [the School of Integrative Healing]. I was looking at my finances and the money wasn't visibly there. Yet I knew, I made a clear decision that the operation was happening and that I was renewing my membership of the school.

It's that moment when we decide within ourselves, it's not making a decision based on current circumstances. Jana talks about making a decision from what you know. I knew I was ready and I followed that intuitive feeling and just trusted that the money would come somehow. At one moment I was worried, there was some stress around the money coming and so I'd sit down and I'd tap into different practices of my own and practices that I've learned with Jana in the school and it happened, the money arrived.

One day I woke up and a client had made a big payment and that began the payments for the membership in the school. I woke up another morning and I was accepted as an ambassador. I was actually going to be working within the school so my membership rate was considerably dropped. It was like I kind of manifested around 7000 euros at that moment. It was just after sitting down and meditating and tapping into the frequency of abundance that I turned on my phone and found out that I'd been accepted as an ambassador. Also, my partner completely and unexpectedly came to me one morning and said he really wanted to contribute to help pay for the operation because he knew how important it was to me. That's when all of the money just flowed in.

I've now had my operation last December and it was the perfect moment in my journey for it to happen. I felt it in my body that removing the implants just made so much sense physically, emotionally, and spiritually, for the way that I can hold space and the way that I can lead by example."

This client's transformational journey is also profound. This is Jessica's story:

"I joined the School of Integrative Healing in 2021, six months after quitting the safety of my job to pursue life working for myself. I had zero income at the time and

truthfully had no clue how to pay for the program. But when I spoke to Jana for the first time I knew in my body that this program had something to offer to change my life. I leaned into every call, every workshop, every practice. Within the next 3 months after joining I had made $12k. Giving me the money to pay for the school and to start to replenish the savings I had been living on since quitting my job. In the next 3 months after that I had made another $20k, giving life and viability to the new journey I was on.

And while the financial success was great at the time, what was better was learning so much about myself that I had avoided and suppressed my entire life. As all of this comes to light it is natural to change, which causes our relationships to change. It brought up all the things in my relationship and put to the forefront the question of 'what do I really want'. This was a question I had rarely asked myself as I was always a people pleaser. But asserting my desires for my life caused my partner and I to ask 'Are we on the same page?' And there was a point I wasn't sure we would make it. But standing in the sureness of myself led him to meet me because I was no longer split on my desires. Eight months later I married the love of my life and we are on the road to creating the exact life I have always wanted for myself. All of this work has given me the foundation I need to keep growing, keep stretching, keep creating, and keep loving."

Sustaining Your Manifestation Journey

Imagine you have just planted a beautiful garden. Initially, you water it daily, weeding, and ensuring it gets just the right amount of sunlight. Over time, as your garden begins to flourish, you realize it requires new types of care—perhaps a bit of shade, different nutrients, or even re-planting in new soil to continue its growth. Like this garden, your manifestation journey is a living, evolving adventure. It thrives on continuous learning and the flexibility to adapt to new conditions. The rest of this chapter is about nurturing that journey, ensuring that your skills and approaches to manifestation evolve as beautifully and resiliently as any well-tended garden.

The Importance of Continuous Learning And Adaptation In Manifestation

Manifestation is not a static skill but a dynamic process that grows and changes with you. As you evolve, so do your dreams, circumstances, and the tools you need to manifest effectively. It is about staying open to new methodologies, ideas, and techniques that can enhance your ability to attract your desires into your life.

Regularly incorporating new knowledge into your manifestation practices is not just beneficial; it is essential. This could mean attending workshops, reading new books on spiritual growth, or even enrolling in online courses that explore advanced manifestation techniques. Each of these activities plays an essential role in enriching your understanding and keeping you engaged in your personal growth journey. For instance, a workshop might introduce you to a new meditation technique that enhances your visualization skills, or a book might offer a different perspective on gratitude that deepens your daily practice.

Other Useful Techniques To Assist In Manifesting Your Goals:

Here are some other modalities I used throughout my journey to help me overcome my struggles. In the School of Integrative Healing, you will have unlimited access to some of these additional training and much more:

- **Holistic Nutrition:** I turned to this after years of eating disorders that led to a very depleted body. Your body cannot function optimally without optimal nutrition. For example, our happy & motivational neurotransmitters in the brain are made from amino acids. I later discovered this had its limitations too. I learned that many health problems are caused by unconscious programs or repressed emotions. So just looking at nutrition is like trying to empty a bath by taking glasses of water out. Healing the root cause program is like turning the tap off and pulling the plug out.

- **The Medicine Wheel** - Spirit of the Inca (by Chris Waters). Chris teaches shamanism and energy work. This was the first time I was given tools to change my programming and heal trauma (personal & ancestral) and start working with energy. It works because it goes to the cause and clears at the root. It also gave me a map to healing, and the language to understand my experiences. Here I was introduced to the four planes: Physical, emotional and mental, spiritual, and energy.

- **The Emotion code** is an energy healing technique by Dr Bradley Nelson that teaches how to identify and release trapped emotions. I discovered this through my experience of adopting a traumatized dog, as all other methods of trauma healing involve language. For a long time, I used the EC for both Maia (my dog) and myself every week to clear emotions and "un-stuck" our nervous systems. The nervous system can get stuck in fight and flight because of trapped experiences or emotions in the body. This modality made a big difference.

- **Thinking into results** with Bob Proctor, the king of manifestation and thought work. It is easy to want modalities and workshops to save you. Bob reminds you that you have to take responsibility for what you are thinking and feeling in the moment. I believe in both: transformation processes, and awareness in the mundane moments.

- **Integrative Quantum Medicine** (Louise Mita): This is a natural non-invasive method of energy medicine used to release blockages. I was feeling very exposed when I started building a business online. IQM protected me energetically from other people's opinions—It is one of the strongest energy modalities I know. It helped my dog with his arthritis. This technique is also great for increasing soul connection.

- **Rapid Resolution Therapy** (RRT Dr. Jon Connolly): This modality facilitates healing by clearing the mind of negative unconscious programs (like shutting tabs of a computer). This is great when you are stuck in a stress pattern and want to clear something from the root.

Group Manifestation Dynamics: Increasing Power Through Collective Intent

Have you ever felt the uplifting energy when a group comes together for a common purpose? A palpable power in numbers can significantly amplify the results of manifestation efforts. This phenomenon is rooted in the collective consciousness and the shared energy dynamics that emerge when individuals unite with a common intent. Think of it as a choir; each individual may have a beautiful voice, but the harmony creates a captivating performance. Similarly, when you join forces in a manifestation group, the unified focus and energy can produce outcomes that are more significant than what might be possible individually. It can accelerate your personal and collective manifestations and provide a network of support and encouragement, reinforcing the idea that together, we can achieve more than we can alone.

Collective Growth: Expanding Manifestation Journey With Community

The path of personal growth and manifestation is often visualized as a solitary trek, where individual effort and introspection drive the journey forward. However, the power of the community in this process cannot be overstated. Just as a single thread gains strength when woven with others, your personal manifestation efforts can be significantly amplified through a community's collective energy and support. Building or joining a community of like-minded individuals enriches your experience. It provides a platform for shared growth and learning. These communities become safe havens where members can share experiences, celebrate successes, support each other through challenges, and hold the belief for one another when the wobble inevitably comes, effectively multiplying the manifesting power of each individual.

Consider the dynamic within a supportive manifestation community; it is a space where your victories are celebrated, and your setbacks are met with compassion and understanding, not judgment. This environment fosters a sense of belonging and connection, which is crucial for personal growth. Members exchange tips, strategies, and insights, which can be incredibly valuable as you navigate your manifestation path. For instance, you might learn about a new visualization technique that worked wonders for someone else or receive encouragement to persist with your tools when having a wobble. The community acts as a sounding board and a faith booster, keeping you engaged and committed to your goals.

There's a marked difference between being a community that believes in possibility, in contrast to a group that is always complaining about how hard life is. Benjamin Hardy in his book *Willpower Doesn't Work* talks about success is NOT the byproduct of discipline, but the environment that you are in. Surround yourself with people who are achieving huge things, having fun, and utterly grateful for their life and you'll become the next one. Surround yourself with people who have one million excuses for why they fail, and you'll not go anywhere. A big part of manifestation is putting yourself in environments in which it is easy for your desires to grow.

In the School of Integrative Healing, the community aspect is central to our teaching model. Here, students learn about manifestation techniques and participate in group activities that enhance their understanding and application of these practices. For example, group meditations are a regular feature, where collective intentions are set, and the group's unified focus helps deepen the meditation experience for each participant. The shared energy in these sessions often leads to profound insights and heightened manifestations. On top of this success, and possibility is normalized, this is a safe space where you can bring your most audacious goals and no one will say *"Oh that's not possible, who are you to want that?"*. No. Everyone responds *"That's amazing, I love that for you, and I absolutely see it"*, increasing belief and faith, making you even more magnetic.

Another key aspect of the School of Integrative Healing is its emphasis on continuous learning and community engagement beyond the classroom. Alumni are encouraged to stay connected through online forums and return for workshops, keeping the community vibrant and supportive long after students have completed their courses. This ongoing engagement ensures that the learning and mutual support are sustained, helping individuals to continue growing and manifesting effectively in all areas of their lives.

Manifestation In The Future

Manifestation practices will evolve significantly, particularly as advancements in neuroscience and quantum physics continue to unfold. These fields will likely offer more profound insights into how our thoughts and emotions shape our reality. With a growing body of scientific evidence supporting the power of mindfulness and positive thinking, I foresee a future where spiritual leaders, psychologists, and other healthcare professionals recommend these practices as part of a holistic approach to well-being.

The role of the community in manifestation practices is also expected to expand as technology facilitates it. Online platforms and social media have already begun to transform how people connect and share knowledge about manifestation. In the future, I envision an increase in virtual communities where people worldwide can come together to participate in guided visualization sessions, share success stories, and support each other's growth. These communities will provide support and motivation but also help amplify collective energy, making individual and group manifestation efforts more powerful.

In this evolving landscape, staying informed and adaptable is critical. As new technologies and scientific discoveries emerge, they bring fresh perspectives and capabilities to traditional manifestation practices. To stay ahead of the curve, engage continuously with new literature, participate in groups, and take courses exploring the latest spiritual and scientific advancements. This proactive approach ensures that your manifestation practices remain effective, enabling you to harness the full potential of both traditional wisdom and modern innovations.

Creating A Legacy Of Abundance: Manifesting For The Next Generation

When you think about manifestation, it is often through the lens of what it can bring into our lives—success, love, health, and prosperity. But what if you shifted our focus slightly to consider what manifestation can do for us and those who will follow? Imagine planting a garden for enjoyment and for future generations to cherish and cultivate. This is the essence of creating a legacy of abundance through manifestation. This process extends the benefits of your efforts far beyond your own life and into the lives of those who come after you.

The concept of a manifestation legacy is about setting intentions that have long-term impacts, focusing on creating abundance that supports not just individual aspirations but also contributes to collective well-being. It is about thinking big and thinking forward; it is about sustainability and responsibility for the planetary and social systems you are a part of. When you manifest with an awareness of your impact on future generations, you align your actions with the greater good, ensuring that the abundance you attract perpetuates and spreads.

EXERCISE:

Journal on these questions:

- Where have I been limiting myself from having what I actually want?

- What and where do you not allow yourself to receive what you want and how can you change it?

We ask you to reflect on "Where have I been limiting myself from having what I actually want?" to create awareness of where you have been unconsciously blocking yourself from moving forward, or actually receiving what you want. This introspection is helpful as it shifts focus from perceived limitations to taking proactive ownership of choices and behaviors.

Secondly, considering "What and where do I not allow myself to receive, and how can I change it?" directs attention to areas in your life that you can increase your receptivity, in order to allow in more good. This exercise serves as a catalyst for identifying blockages—whether in relationships, career, health, or personal development—and understanding their underlying causes. When you see the pattern, you can choose to change, and that's where your power lies.

Conclusion

As I draw this journey to a close, let's take a moment to reflect on the incredible landscape we have navigated together. From understanding the intricate dance between quantum physics and neuroplasticity to embracing the profound wisdom of spiritual practices, we have explored how the science and art of manifestation are interconnected and two sides of the same coin. This fusion is the heartbeat of our approach, showing us that a balanced perspective enhances our manifestation efforts and empowers us to tap into a wellspring of potential within ourselves.

Remember, the core principles of manifestation are not just theories to be pondered but practical tools for use. Each day offers us a new canvas to apply these techniques—visualizations, breath work, inner child work, or shifting our mindset to the being we want to be so that our outer world can mirror it. Consistency here is your ally; the daily steps, no matter how small, weave the tapestry of your realized dreams. I committed myself to the practices in this book for a year, and that is how everything in my life changed 180 degrees, from being a broke yoga teacher living in India and with chronic health conditions to building easeful natural wealth and a business that I love, to having a healthy body and a thriving relationship with my partner and other incredible results. People around me who knew me in the past could not believe how fast and in the manners my life was changing. They started asking me questions and paying attention to what I was doing. So, do not underestimate the power and velocity this can move when you commit to it.

Indeed, this journey is full of challenges. Doubts may surface, and obstacles (blessings in disguise) may appear in your path. However, these challenges are not indicators of failure; instead, they are opportunities for personal growth leading to even more good. Resistance arises naturally in life, so remain mindful when you encounter it. It may require daily recommitment, and that's perfectly okay. Commitment can be light and fun, especially when you are gentle with yourself.

And remember, every journey is unique—yours will be no different. Treat yourself with kindness, and do not shy away from celebrating every victory along the way, no matter how Fminor they may seem. In fact, tracking your progress on the way to your goal is crucial to your success. Let your own stories inspire you; let them remind you of what is possible when you commit to your manifestation journey. Your story, too, can be one of transformation and triumph.

Now, I encourage you to step forward with the insights and tools you have gained. Whether this is the beginning of your manifestation journey or a point where you are diving deeper, let each practice be a thread in the fabric of a life you are actively creating. Keep learning, keep exploring, and let each discovery bring you closer to the life you aspire to live.

Lastly, remember this: You are immensely powerful. With each thought and intentional action, you are shaping your reality. Hold onto this understanding and let it guide you as you manifest the life of your dreams.

Thank you for allowing me to be a part of your journey. Here is to your success, growth, and limitless potential. Let's continue to manifest miracles together.

With warmth and belief in your boundless capabilities,

Jana Alonso Bartlett

Testimonials From Clients

Jessica P.

"My experience in TSIH has been life changing. I found a woman on the internet who showed me a version of myself I wanted to be. A version that was not afraid to show up and be silly and weird and loud. A version of me that communicated not only with others but with herself. Not being afraid of what they might see, but rather embracing it, alchemizing it. turning it into power."

Jess K.

"Jana has changed my life. Since she entered my life 3 years ago, everything in my life and business has changed. I remember being part of the first round of the school of IH and I was blown away. Finally I had the answers I was looking for. Finally I understood why I was stuck. Finally I saw a light at the end of the tunnel.

2 years after my time in the school I decided to rejoin and I could not be happier. I highly recommend."

Eva S.

"TSIH has truly empowered me to become my own healer and embrace my truest self. As someone who is highly sensitive and has faced frequent exposure to conflict, navigating and processing emotions has always been a challenge. Despite trying various modalities of therapy, I never found a comprehensive solution until I discovered TSIH."

Review

Make a Difference with Your Review and Unlock the Power of Generosity

People who give without expecting anything in return live longer, happier lives and often find more success. Would you help someone you've never met, even if you never got credit for it?

Who is this person you ask? They're like you. Or, at least, like you used to be. Less experienced, wanting to make a difference, and needing help, but not sure where to look. Our mission is to make the teachings of manifestation accessible to everyone. Everything we do stems from that mission. And, the only way for us to accomplish that mission is by reaching...well...everyone.

This is where you come in. Most people do judge a book by its cover (and its reviews). My ask on behalf of a person struggling to manifest their dreams, someone you've never met: Please help that person by leaving this book a review. Your gift costs no money and less than 60 seconds to make real, but can change a fellow reader's life forever. Your review could help...

...one more small business provide for their community

....one more entrepreneur support their family.

...one more employee get meaningful work.

...one more client transform their life.

...one more dream come true.

All you have to do is, and it takes less than 60 seconds, to leave a review.

Simply scan the QR code below to leave your review:

https://link.manifestwitheasebook.com/PaperReview

Thank you from the bottom of my heart. I'm excited to help you achieve your dreams faster and easier than you can imagine. You'll love the techniques and strategies I'm about to share in the coming chapters.

Now, back to our regularly scheduled programming.

- Your biggest fan, Jana Alonso Bartlett

References

- Haque, B. (2023, December 12). A quantum physics explanation of manifestation and law of attraction: It's not BS. *Imperium* *Publication*. https://www.imperiumpublication.com/post/a-quantum-phy sics-explanation-of-manifestation-and-law-of-attraction-it-s-n ot-bs

- Angel, H.-F.,& Seitz, R. J. (2016). Processes of believing: Where do they come from? What are they good for? *Frontiers in Psychology*, *7*, 302. https://www.ncbi.nlm.nih.gov/pmc/articles/PMC5200943/

- *How gratitude changes you and your brain*. (n.d.). Greater Good. https://greatergood.berkeley.edu/article/item/how_gratitude _changes_you_and_your_brain

- Neuroq. (2023, July 10). The psychology and effectiveness of manifesting. *Psychology Today*. Retrieved July 16, 2024, from https://www.psychologytoday.com/us/blog/experimentation s/202307/the-psychology-and-effectiveness-of-manifesting

- Grohol, J. M. (2009, December 15). Seeing is believing: The power of visualization. *Psychology Today*. Retrieved July 16, 2024, from https://www.psychologytoday.com/us/blog/flourish/200912/seeing-is-believing-the-power-visualization

- Lipton, B. H. (2005). *The Biology of Belief: Unleashing the Power of consciousness, matter, & Miracles.* Hay House.

- *Becoming divine.* (n.d.-b). https://drjoedispenza.com/dr-joes-blog/becoming-divine

- Richter, F. (2023, July 3). Apple's road to $3 trillion. *Statista Daily Data*. https://www.statista.com/chart/14953/apple-market-capitalization/

- *Rapid Resolution Therapy®.* (n.d.). Rapid Resolution Therapy®. https://rapidresolutiontherapy.com/

- Katie, B., & Mitchell, S. (2002). *Loving What Is: Four questions that can change your life.* Harmony Books.

- Dr. Brad :). (n.d.). *Dr. Bradley Nelson – The personal side.* Dr. Bradley Nelson. https://drbradleynelson.com/

- *Spirit of the Inca.* (n.d.). https://spiritoftheinca.com/

- *Tao Energy - Louise Mita.* (n.d.). The Art of Energy. https://www.taoenergy.com/

- Green, T. (Producer), Baylin, Z. (Writer), & Marcus, R. (Director). (2021). King Richard [Film]. Warner Bros. Pictures.

- ANF Therapy. (n.d.). Retrieved July 10, 2024, from https://www.anftherapy.com/

- Maltz, M. (1960). *Psycho-cybernetics: A new way to get more living out of life*. Prentice-Hall.

- Hardy, B. (2018). *Willpower doesn't work: Discover the hidden keys to success*. Hachette Books.

Made in the USA
Coppell, TX
07 October 2024

38294488R00075